Rollo's Way

Also by Nicholas Hasluck

Novels

Quarantine
The Blue Guitar
The Hand That Feeds You
The Bellarmine Jug
Truant State
The Country Without Music
The Blosseville File
A Grain of Truth
Our Man K
Arbella's Baby
Dismissal
Rooms in the City
The Bradshaw Case

Short Stories

The Hat on the Letter O
Wobbling the Whiteboard

Essays and Memoirs

Collage
Offcuts from a Legal Literary Life
Light That Time Has Made (ed.)
The Chance of Politics (ed.)
The Legal Labyrinth
Somewhere in the Atlas
Legal Limits
The Hasluck Banner
Jigsaw: Patterns in Law and Literature
Beyond the Equator: A Memoir

Poetry

Anchor and Other Poems
On the Edge
Chinese Journey
A Dream Divided

Nicholas Hasluck

Rollo's Way

Rollo's Way
ISBN 978 1 76041 930 1
Copyright © Nicholas Hasluck 2020
Cover photo: the author with his brother Rollo in schooldays

First published 2020 by
GINNINDERRA PRESS
PO Box 3461 Port Adelaide 5015
www.ginninderrapress.com.au

Contents

Beginning	9
Prac	18
Another School	31
Canberra Days	41
Another Shot	49
The Early Sixties	57
Moving On	75
Dartmouth Days	90
Visions and Investments	105
Government Houses	112
Back to Business	133
The Next Phase	144
Ending	158

For R

You do not lie in death alone
For some of me went with you there
And rests forever where you rest.
And you walk with me everywhere.
Thus I, still living, not alone
Will often share with you,
Still bright and active, ever here,
Memories of all we used to do.
In loneliness but not distress
I draw from stores of happiness
Not only consolation but a breath
Of your quick self beyond the body's death.

Paul Hasluck

Beginning

It is often rewarding in a quiet moment to recall times spent with some of those who have passed on but are still dear to us. This is true especially of an older brother, so I am minded to set down some recollections of my brother Rollo: his zest, his humour, his way of going at things full bore. I trust that Rollo's story will not only be of interest to his family circle but also to those with an interest in times past and a feeling for the way it is between brothers, that special bond.

Rollo was born in Perth on 15 January 1941, the first child of a West Australian couple, Paul and Alexandra Hasluck. It was a heatwave day with bushfires burning in King's Park within sight of his mother's hospital window. His mother, generally called Alix, had been a teacher but was now looking after the family home at 2 Adams Road, Claremont. This was built on land bought by Paul and Alix a few years before Rollo's birth. It was a single-storeyed residence, art deco style, in a cul-de-sac overlooking Freshwater Bay, a stretch of the Swan River lying halfway between the city of Perth and the port of Fremantle. In those days, Rollo's father was a journalist with *The West Australian* newspaper.

Paul and Alix had grown up in Perth and completed their education at the University of Western Australia. In addition to other achievements, they were both destined to become well-known writers and, in later life, both published autobiographies. These books – *Mucking About* by Paul Hasluck and *Portrait in a Mirror* by Alexandra Hasluck – describe their early years and family lineage. The books are there for reference if required, so I will pass over such matters lightly.

It appears from *Portrait in a Mirror* that Alix's father, John Darker, was an engineer from Queensland who had come to Perth in the gold rush era. He died mid-career, while Alix was still young, so the full name given to her first child, with a nod to her paternal background, was Rollo John Darker Hasluck. The name Darker is said to come from a French family called d'Arques which moved to England after the Norman Conquest. Rollo was named after a forebear of this family, Rollo the Northman, who is said to have brought peace to his province.

There was no peace to be had in Perth in early 1941. Soon after Rollo's birth, as a consequence of the Australian war effort, Paul Hasluck left his job at *The West Australian* to join the Department of External Affairs in Canberra. While Paul went off to Canberra to look for accommodation, Alix stayed in Perth to see to the letting of the house at 2 Adams Road. She was then ready for the train trip to the east coast with the baby, a dog called Dora, and her mother, Evelyn Darker.

This was wartime. The train and the platform at Perth station were crowded with khaki-clad figures. Amidst the confusion, by the time Alix had found some water for the dog and shouted farewell to a gaggle of friends who had gathered to see them off, suddenly, above the bustle and frantic commotion, came a shriek, 'The baby. Take the baby.' Panic! She had forgotten Rollo! The baby was passed through the window, the train pulled out, and off they went.

The Haslucks' first house in Canberra was at 8 Furneaux Street, Deakin, close to the shops at Manuka. In the years that followed, after her mother had returned to Perth, Alix procured the services of a succession of part-time maids, each of whom, it appears from *Portrait in a Mirror*, were remembered principally for their amiable eccentricities. For example, if Alix asked Isobel to get Rollo up after his afternoon nap, the local girl would rush into the room, fling up the blind with a crash, while shouting to the sleeping cherub in the cot, 'Gunna get up, mate?' Thus aroused, the nappy-clad infant would scramble to the end of the cot with what Alix described as 'a gorgeous toothless smile'.

Alix added to the story in this way:

> One of the few recollections I have of the Furneaux Street house before we left it was of going into the dining room one winter's

night to find Paul in front of the fire with Rollo beside him on a rug. Paul was reading Milton's poem 'Paradise Lost' to him.

'Whatever are you doing?' I said. 'He can't understand it.'

'No, but he likes it,' said my husband, and then, 'Don't you think he has a tragic look in the eyes?'

'Don't be silly,' I said. But as things turned out, he could have seen more than I did.

There were other peculiarities in Canberra at this time. After the fall of Singapore in early 1942, the local citizenry prepared for Japanese bombing attacks by putting up blackout curtains and criss-crossing mirrors with sticky tape to guard against flying glass. Everyone was busy digging air-raid shelters and laying in what supplies they could.

The Haslucks then moved to another rented property near Manuka at 6 Grant Street, Deakin. To save travel costs, Paul acquired a thoroughbred mare called Edythe. He rode her over to his office at West Block, where the External Affairs Department was situated, and tethered her on the slopes of Camp Hill, behind Parliament House. Later in that year, Rollo acquired a younger brother – Nicholas, generally called Nick – for I was born at Allawah Hospital, Canberra, on 17 October 1942.

Towards the end of World War II, as head of the Post-Hostilities Section of the Department, Paul Hasluck joined the Australian delegation to the San Francisco conference where the United Nations was formed. The delegation was led by the Deputy Prime Minister, Frank Forde, and the mercurial Minister for External Affairs, Dr H.V. Evatt. A year or so later, in March 1946, Paul was appointed Head of the Australian Mission to the United Nations. He left Canberra immediately to attend some early sessions of the UN in New York.

The arrangements made for Alix to join her husband in due course included a train journey to Brisbane with her two infant sons, a voyage to San Francisco on the *Mariposa* – one of several so-called 'bride ships' carrying young Australian wives of American servicemen to the United States – followed by a cross-country train journey to New York with a group of public servants from Canberra. This group was led by one of

Paul's contemporaries in the department, Arthur Tange. Arthur's wife Marjorie Tange was known to Alix from their schooldays at Perth College.

When their train pulled into New York Grand Central, Paul and other Australians were there to meet the newcomers. Paul drove his wife and two small sons to their new family home at Bronxville (not to be confused with the Bronx) on the edge of Westchester County, about half an hour out of Manhattan Island. The double-storeyed rented house was on Boulder Trail, just off Highland Circle, not far from the Bronxville station. It emerges from Paul's book of reminiscences *Diplomatic Witness* and from Alix's *Portrait in a Mirror* that both of Rollo's parents were soon caught up in a busy round of official engagements.

Their various commitments are fully described in their books so, again, I will pass over the details. It will be enough to say that as the Australian representative on the Security Council of the UN at this time, Paul was much in demand. The Security Council, after its initial meeting at Church House in London earlier in the year, was now meeting at Hunter College in the Bronx. Paul's office was in the Empire State Building – midtown Manhattan – on the forty-fifth floor, about halfway up the famous structure. One of my earliest childhood memories is standing with Rollo in my father's office, side by side, as we edged forward to the window and peered at the traffic way down below: tiny automobiles like miniature toys – mostly yellow taxicabs – shifting and surging along Fifth Avenue.

I gather from my parents' books that Rollo went to the Bronxville Public School and a place was found for me at the nursery school of Sarah Lawrence College, which was just up the road from our new home at Boulder Trail. I thus have some claim to being an old boy of what at that time was one of the most famous, exclusively female colleges in North America!

Our attendance at schools in the area led to Paul and Alix forming a friendship with the Bryan family living nearby, and to Rollo becoming a buddy of their son, Samuel Bryan. Our family scrapbook covering the years in New York has a number of photos of Rollo and me in the Bryan swimming pool during the summer months, buoyed up in the water by inflated tyre tubes. There are also photos of us in our fur-lined snowsuits in winter, standing in a whitened streetscape beneath leafless trees.

I will digress to say that many years later, while attending a legal conference in New York, my wife Sally and I, with our two sons, Anthony and Lindsay, went to some of the places that Rollo and I had been to as boys – the Empire State Building, for example, and the Statue of Liberty. Also, we took a trip to Westchester County to see the double-storeyed house at Boulder Trail, with its row of dormer windows, which was once the Hasluck family home.

Even later, in 2018, while Sally and I were renting a flat in Greenwich Village for a few weeks, I caught a train to Bedford Park in the Bronx to have a look at Hunter College where my father Paul had served as a member of the Security Council. Upon reading a plaque by the main hall, I discovered that the campus had been renamed and is now known as Lehman College: to commemorate the career of Herbert H. Lehman, who had served as a governor of New York and US senator. Another plaque established that 'the Security Council met here, the first home of the United Nations, March 25 – August 15, 1946'.

Paul Hasluck observed in *Diplomatic Witness* that, during the war years, the college had been taken over by the navy. It was then used as a temporary home for the UN until the owners sought return of their property. Another temporary home for the UN was found in the Henry Hudson Hotel in 57th Street, Manhattan. A third temporary home was provided by converting part of a great factory at Lake Success on Long Island.

Eventually, due to the generosity of the Rockefeller family, a permanent home for the body was established on Manhattan Island by the East River. My online research revealed that it wasn't worth visiting the former site of the UN at Lake Success. The premises in question – a base for the Sherry Gyroscope Plant on Marcus Avenue – had long since been replaced by massive residential condominiums and shopping malls.

But in the early days of the United Nations in the 1940s, most of the social events were held in midtown Manhattan. Alix's reminiscences in *Portrait in a Mirror* include a description of a reception by the Australian Society in New York for the showing of the film *The Overlanders* starring Chips Rafferty, one of the best and most evocative films of wartime Australia.

After the first formal showing, the film went in to the commercial cinemas, and one day she decided to take her two young sons to see it, thinking they should know what their homeland was like. They sat rapt with attention.

When it came to the point where the girl swims her horse across a creek and a crocodile rears its ugly snout in pursuit, Rollo shouted excitedly, 'Look out! Look out for the croc!'

All the heads nearby quickly turned. Alligators are the American saurian and Rollo's was an Australian voice. Alix didn't think it did the audience any harm to catch on that this was not a film about some outlying part of America.

It seems that on another day Paul telephoned Alix from Lake Success on Long Island, where the UN was now meeting, and asked her to drive over and fetch him. He felt so ill he couldn't go back to his office in the Empire State building. So she put her sons in their best coats and reached the Security Council meeting at five-fifty p.m., just as the Russian envoy Andre Gromyko was making a shattering statement about the atom bomb.

She continues in this way:

> I'm afraid we completely stole his thunder. As we walked into the front row of the section for Distinguished Visitors, heads were turning away from the rostrum and everyone was whispering. 'What darling little English boys!' Even most of the delegates were watching us as they had often heard me mention the boys at dinner parties, it being a nice safe topic. They were both wearing dark green tailored tweed overcoats and long grey socks, their fair hair slicked, and their eyes alight with interest; very different from the get-up of most American children.

It emerges from *Diplomatic Witness* that, in April 1947, after a falling out with his minister, the incorrigible Dr Evatt, Paul resigned from the Department of External Affairs with a view to returning to Western Australia. While waiting for a ship to make the trip home Alix took her two sons by train to the home of a distant cousin in Jacksonville, Florida, being joined by Paul a few weeks later. Photos in the scrapbook show Rollo and me in the front garden of our relative's home in various forms of fancy dress.

Our weird costumes may have been prompted by the stories we heard read aloud in Florida, for I still have on my shelves copies of books presented to us by my distant cousin Bruce Rhodes shortly before we left: *Alice in Wonderland* and *Alice Through the Looking Glass*. These have wonderful sketches of the White Rabbit, Tweedledum and Tweedledee, Alice at the Mad Hatter's tea party and a picture of Alice nibbling the mushroom that kept changing her size from very large to very small.

A few weeks later, with Paul behind the wheel of our large black Chevrolet, the family set off on a sightseeing excursion by road that took us first to New Orleans, then northwards through Louisiana, Alabama and Georgia. The Smoky Mountains of Tennessee and North Carolina were a treat. We went on to Virginia, Maryland and Pennsylvania. The family scrapbooks are a jumble of postcards, brochures and photos of Rollo and me at all sorts of fascinating places, from alligator farms in Florida to the stockade forts at Williamsburg and the reconstitution of Sir Walter Raleigh's former colony at Roanoak.

Our parents had been hoping that at the end of this meandering road trip we would board a boat for Australia. Not so. The sailing date was unexpectedly cancelled, so they had to find a place to stay for another month.

In a letter dated 26 June 1947 to his old friend at the University of Western Australia, Professor Fred Alexander, Paul wrote,

> We couldn't manage another month of touring and in any case the children, whose interest in sightseeing is sporadic, and highly specialised in favour of Red Indians and automobile crashes, would

probably have renounced their parents if we suggested more travelling. So we settled for Cape Cod, found a most agreeable boarding house with a pleasant family of New Englanders at Buzzard's Bay near the base of the Cape. We stayed there until a few days ago, except for a few excursions to Boston and New Bedford and other places in the locality.

I am reminded by this letter that while at Buzzard's Bay, from rocks strewn about the place, Rollo and I, with our father's help, built an impressive rock fort looking out to sea. It had a roughly-shaped window from which to observe the approach of piratical marauders. Alix noted in *Portrait in a Mirror* that Rollo slightly marred things by getting poison ivy blisters all over him. It was very painful and the only treatment known was to scrub the blisters daily with harsh yellow soap.

Back in New York, we stayed briefly at the Forest Hills Inn, Forest Hills, before boarding our ship, the *Port Chalmers*, which was berthed at Brooklyn, Long Island. We sailed at midnight on 1 July, on our way to Brisbane via the Panama Canal, with no ports of call. As the ship moved slowly through the canal, Rollo and I were fascinated by the boys on the neighbouring docks diving for coins thrown over the rail by passengers, often in matchboxes to keep the coin afloat long enough for retrieval.

There were quite a few children aboard and our scrapbook photos suggest there were a good many fancy dress parties in the course of the voyage. Our youthful fellow travellers included a migrant Jewish family with a lively daughter of Rollo's age called Eve. She became well-known in the 1970s as Eve Mahlab, a leading figure in the Australian Women's Electoral Lobby, a founder of a Melbourne-based lawyers' recruiting agency – Eve Mahlab and Associates – and eventually an Australian Businesswoman of the Year.

Not so long ago, I invited Eve and her husband to dinner at our home in Perth, which led to sharing memories of our childhood voyage to Australia aboard the *Port Chalmers*. I recall especially, as I am sure Rollo did too, the special moment when our parents took us on deck at dawn for a first glimpse of the Australian coastline on the approach to Brisbane. We could certainly sense their excitement at the thought of coming home after several years abroad.

Upon returning to the family home at 2 Adams Road, overlooking Freshwater Bay at Claremont, it wasn't long before we all settled into a regular pattern. Paul was completing a book about his time at the United Nations – *Workshop of Security* – and had been commissioned to contribute two volumes to the series comprising the official Australian war history. They were published eventually under the title *The Government and the People 1939–1945*.

Paul spent a good deal of time on the UWA campus but was usually available towards the end of an afternoon for walks along the foreshore of Freshwater Bay with his two sons. He taught us to skim stones on the still surface of the river at that hour and on some occasions would chat to members of prawning parties who were laying out their nets before nightfall. Alix had to keep an eye on her ageing mother, who lived at 51 Clifton Crescent, Mount Lawley, but still found time to reconnect with various friends including her closest companion, the well-known writer Henrietta Drake-Brockman, who lived with her husband Geoffrey Drake-Brockman at Lawson Flats in the city.

I can't quite recall whether in this, the first phase of our return, Rollo joined me in finger-painting and other messy pursuits at the small redbrick kindergarten on the corner of Beatrice Road and Jutland Parade, just below the courts of the Dalkeith Tennis Club – a building which is still there after all these years – but it certainly wasn't long before we were both attending the East Claremont Primary School. This was generally called 'Prac School' because it adjoined the Claremont Teachers College and was known as a place where trainee teachers could practise their skills.

Prac

A history of the East Claremont Practising School – *Prac* by Michael Berson – shows that I was enrolled at the school in 1948 but, curiously, the list of enrolments doesn't include Rollo. This suggests that he may have entered the school towards the end of the 1947 school year when the enrolment list for that year had been finalised. This seems likely, because he was six years of age by then while I was probably still young enough to be packed off to kindergarten for a few months, before joining him at Prac in February, at the start of the school year.

It appears from the school history that 'by the mid-1940s Prac had regained its pre-eminence as the top primary school in the State'. It seems that the school had to provide 'for over 200 children' and also 'for a large part of the professional training of students for the Training College'.

Prac was a friendly place and within walking distance from our home at 2 Adams Road. Our daily route took us to Parker Road, across a corner of College Park, along a stretch of Bay Road overshadowed by a double line of majestic sugar gum trees, then to the cluster of school buildings on the corner of Bay Road and Princess Avenue. The cluster included a weatherboard building with a small front veranda known as the 'Rural School'. This was a replica of the sort of school that freshly minted teachers were bound to encounter when assigned to country towns in the wheatbelt (or even further afield) after graduation. A large blackboard with a sill for stubs of white chalk dominated the classroom, overlooking the rows of small brown wooden desks.

Various friends and classmates are mentioned in the school history, including many of those we kept in touch with in later life: Elizabeth King, Michael Beech, Hubert and Roger Day, Dennis and Ted Culley,

Norman Sudlow, Richard Peploe, Graham Davies, John Laney, Rob Nunn, John Malloch, Colin Thorpe, Ian Ward, Charles Moody, Paul Newton, Kevin Somes and so on.

One marvels at the range of careers that were pursued in later life by some of the students at Prac in that early post-war period: Bob Nicholson became a Federal Court judge, Jeffrey Michaels an internationally acclaimed violinist, Ian Temby a federal Director of Public Prosecutions, Peter Smedley a leading Australian businessman, Jack Harrison an editor of Perth's afternoon paper the *Daily News*, Colin Mayrhofer a professor of Classics at the Australian National University, Ken Freeman a world-famous astronomer based at Mount Stromlo. One of the most impressive teachers at Prac in our time was Douglas Jecks, fresh from the adjoining training college, roaming the classroom with an abundance of youthful vitality. He went on to become vice-chancellor of Edith Cowan University.

All of this lay in the future but, looking back, one can see a few straws in the wind. Ken Freeman, the eventual astronomer, lived just around the corner from us. He was interested in telescopes and the night sky even then. On his back lawn one evening, he pointed out Orion's Belt. It was he who sealed off a portion of his parents' garage to create a mysterious 'dark room'. He invited Rollo and me to assist him in developing the output of our box camera. Beneath the hazy glow of a light bulb covered with red cloth, we would watch the ghostly images assume their final form in his tray of chemicals, before the dripping prints were pegged out to dry on a sagging clothesline strung from one side of the room to the other. Rollo reciprocated by inviting Ken to join our team of so-called 'hell-riders' who were addicted to careering down the slope of Adams Road on bikes or hill trolleys to plunge into the long grass and bamboo patches on the foreshore of Freshwater Bay.

Margaret Anketell lived directly opposite our home at 2 Adams Road with her mother, Madge Anketell, a war widow. Margaret was a little older than Rollo but already with aspirations to be an actress, as she did indeed become in later years. The Anketell household was principally renowned in the street for turning on the annual Guy Fawkes night fireworks display in their inner courtyard, under the supervision of Margaret's much older brother, Ken Anketell. He was training to be an engineer but also was a would-be magician, which probably explained his skill in laying out rockets and Roman candles and in pinning Catherine wheels to wooden boards where, after dark, to the great delight of the assembled throng they would spin crazily, surrounded by little kids waving sparklers.

It was Margaret who slipped an anonymous note into the Hasluck letter box on one occasion inviting Rollo and me to attend the inaugural meeting of an as yet unnamed secret society, a get together to be held after dark behind the bamboo patch on the foreshore. With bated breath, we found our way to the designated rendezvous, but were not entirely surprised to find that the theatrically minded Margaret was the convenor of the meeting. She was sitting there by candlelight with her friend from nearby Watkins Road, Fay Hamling, wearing dark glasses and with a French-style blue beret sloping across her brow.

It turned out that Margaret hadn't been able to recruit anyone else to what was now to be known as the Dead Bird Society, but she wasn't discouraged. In addition to putting on a show for amateur magicians at Assembly Hall in the city, her enterprising brother had picked up an operative film camera from somewhere. So Margaret decided to make a movie. She recruited some school friends, assigned the principal role to herself and looked to Rollo and me, her faithful Dead Bird Society members, to fill in some of the minor parts.

The story line underpinning Margaret's makeshift script was something to do with espionage, as a result of which the Hasluck brothers, dressed up in scout uniforms, supposedly as stalwarts of a local youth movement, waved hurricane lanterns to and fro on the foreshore beneath Margaret's house in response to the presence of invading vessels in the bay. I can't quite recall whether we were supposed to be good guys warning the defence forces of what was afoot or bad guys (a kind of Hitler Youth) secretly and disgracefully showing the enemy where to land.

Margaret showed the film eventually to a small audience of friends and relatives seated around a white sheet serving as a screen in the Anketell garage. I recall the thrill of being there and watching our lantern waving, with a close-up of Rollo using one hand to shade his eyes as he stared at the bay (unless it was meant to be a salute or secret signal of some kind) but I fear that most of the audience, although generally appreciative, couldn't quite gather what was going on.

Margaret's script was possibly influenced by the serials and B-grade movies being shown at Saturday afternoon matinees at the time. In this, the pre-television era, there were picture theatres in all the suburbs around Freshwater Bay – the Dalkeith cinema in Waratah Avenue, the art deco Windsor Theatre on Stirling Highway (rendered special, with a nod to Hollywood, by a couple of palm trees near the entrance), the Claremont Theatre with its Chinese-themed outdoor picture gardens, plus the Swanbourne and Mosman Park cinemas. But I am inclined to think, on the whole, that Margaret probably drew more upon her active imagination and personal circumstances.

The front lawn of the Anketell property provided a fine view of Freshwater Bay. An undeveloped quarter-acre below the lawn ran down to bull rushes and an old wooden fence at the water's edge. To stand on Margaret's lawn at sunset, with yachts and the occasional launch in silhouette against the western sky, was always an enchanting experience.

Ken Anketell had an old-fashioned yacht moored just offshore. At dusk, to my boyish gaze, this boat, with its sloping sails, resembled a sloop or mysterious pearling lugger. Now and again, we were invited to join the Anketells and some of their friends on a cruise to the far side of the bay as the light fell. Ken and one of his friends would attend to the tiller and the sails while those at the back of the boat joined in the singing of well-known songs such as 'Waltzing Matilda' or 'Irene Good Night'.

Rollo and I lost touch with Margaret as the years went by and our lives took us in different directions. She became an actress and, after a successful career in the world of British theatre in the 1960s, returned to Perth, where she was often seen in local productions. Some years ago, she contacted me to say that she and her husband were making arrangements to scatter her brother's ashes on the surface of Freshwater Bay, below their former home. When she called in to discuss this and some legal issues about the estate, it emerged that she herself, after a full life, had a terminal condition and was close to the end. In talking about old times, she mentioned a couple of things that may have had a bearing on the movie she had made with her brother's camera so many years ago.

Her father, Lieutenant Colonel Anketell, had served on the Western Front in the Great War and was called into service again at the start of World War II. He was commanding Australian troops during the defence of Singapore but didn't return. Before he left for service overseas, according to Margaret, he cautioned his wife and children about the risk of a Japanese invasion and the need for resistance. It seems he had in his possession a Vickers machine gun which was still workable. He instructed his son Ken in the use of it.

On the vacant quarter-acre block sloping down to the foreshore from their front lawn a makeshift 'training area' was set up. It was here that Margaret, by handling the ammunition belt, combined with her brother in firing the machine gun at a target on the slope so they would know how to use it, if necessary. To the best of her recollection, some of the firing was done with blanks but certainly some real bullets were used. It came as a surprise to me, and it certainly would have come as a great surprise to Rollo, to learn that a machine gun had been put to use at the bottom of our generally quiet suburban street.

Margaret laughed about this as the conversation ran on and about some other equally surreal moments, including the occasion at the Assembly Hall in Pier Street when she was supposedly sawn in half on stage while cooperating with her brother as a magician's assistant. This wasn't his only trick. In the family living room, with a black hood over his face, Ken would identify a card selected by a member of the audience as the queen of hearts or the king of clubs or whatever. Years later, upon moving out of their home, Margaret discovered wires laid under a rug from the arm rest of the chair usually occupied by her mother to the place where the hooded Ken usually stood, ready to receive a coded signal of some sort.

Unfortunately, this brief but enjoyable reunion with Margaret turned out to be our last get-together. Having scattered her brother's ashes, she died soon afterwards.

To speak of Freshwater Bay in those other times is to be reminded of what my father said about the Swan River while recalling what it meant to him:

> Much of my own personal happiness is linked with that river, I have paddled in it, fished, crabbed, prawned, rowed, sailed and swum in it and wandered along its banks watching birds or camping under its paper-barks and she-oaks. Those old friends who grew up in the same generation are closer friends because of our common experience as boys and youths on the river and because of our common store of remembered happiness. Through stories told in the family, I feel that I have known the river for a hundred years and love to trace where people lived and what happened long before my time.

Rollo and I shared the feelings my father Paul described. In our early years at school, running through to the 1950s, we too fished and sailed and crabbed, mostly on Freshwater Bay. We learnt to swim at Claremont Baths, an old stockade (long since demolished) connected to the river bank at the foot of Chester Road by a wooden pier, with Claremont Jetty and Claremont Yacht Club only a short distance away to the west. For a time during our schooldays, Rollo and I walked daily along the foreshore of the bay in the summer months to attend training sessions at the baths. On hot afternoons, we joined our friends from Prac and other schools in the fenced-off enclosure beneath an old grey diving tower, adding our bit to the mayhem in the main pool, while yachts in the background, spinnakers aloft, cruised towards Point Walter on the far side of the Bay or shouldered their way home to the Claremont Yacht Club or to the Freshwater Bay Yacht Club at Keane's Point in Peppermint Grove.

The main pool was an open-air, saltwater tub churned up by the kickings and thrashings of countless youthful limbs: a shout-filled, splash-strewn place inhabited by freestyle-crawlers, side-strokers, backstrokers, dog-paddlers, duck-divers, deadman-floaters, barnacle-collectors and also by many would-be champions who kept on swimming from one end of the main pool to the other, trying to ignore the rabble.

Larrikins from the beer garden at the nearby Hotel Continental would sometimes come down to join in the mayhem. They strutted and swaggered along the wooden sidewalks of the enclosure, pushing each other in, doing bombshells off the diving tower, lobbying a jellyfish or two over the high partition which separated the main pool from the smaller girls' pool, guffawing as they listened to the shrieks. Yes, Claremont Baths had something for everyone, and everyone came.

The lessees of the baths at this time were initially the Pederson family. They were followed by Arthur Howson and his wife, a family which included a number of well-known local swimming champions. Rollo and I were coached by Arthur Howson. Percy Oliver, who had won a silver medal for backstroke at the 1936 Olympics in Berlin, was a popular figure at the baths. He gave lessons to novices and trained some of the older swimmers who competed in the races held by the Claremont Swimming Club on Tuesday nights in the summer months.

Claremont Jetty was another place to go. Rowing boats could be hired from a stall at the foot of jetty road, made or repaired perhaps at the Mews family boat shed nearby. From time to time, on weekends, my father hired a boat for an hour or so and took us fishing. Our garage at home housed a bundle of scoop nets – poles with wire mesh baskets attached to one end – which could be used for scooping up blue manna crabs. We would trawl through the shallows from just below Adams Road to the Mews boat shed, then back again. We always had to wear sandshoes to avert the possibility of stepping on a cobbler. I did so on one occasion and the agony caused by the venom from its sting was unbearable.

After some guidance from our father, we became skilled at catching crabs with drop nets from the end of Claremont Jetty. It was pleasing to be there at nightfall on a still summer evening and to watch the lights come on across the bay. The surface of the water stretching outwards from the jetty towards Point Walter would begin glimmering faintly with slivers of golden light, as if from shore to shore, until the time came to use our hurricane lanterns, so we could handle the catch safely when we raised our nets, battling the feisty claws.

It was in these years also that my father used to take Rollo and me across to Subiaco for horse riding lessons at the Acme Riding School. My father had been brought up in the country and, as indicated by his habit of riding to work on his mare Edythe in Canberra during the war, a love of horses stayed with him throughout his life. He was keen to see his sons replicate his skills. The Acme premises consisted of a cluster of stables and related facilities at the western end of Hay Street in Subiaco, close to the underpass crossing beneath the Perth/Fremantle railway line.

We began by riding docile horses around a sawdust-filled ring within the Acme premises, a ring enclosed by roughly hewn wooden barriers. But it wasn't long before our instructor was leading us and other youthful riders through the underpass to the open areas below Reabold Hill, bushland at that time but destined to become part of the gradually expanding residential suburbs of Daglish and Jolimont. The Acme Riding School and its little arena have long since disappeared, being taken over by a hardware store eventually, but we were left with some pleasant memories of making our way through the waterlogged terrain at the foot of Reabold Hill – now known as Perry Lakes – and the sense of adventure that always accompanies a journey on horseback.

In addition to riding, Paul was keen for us to have some experience of the Australian bush. He took us camping on the Murray River and at Lake Leschenaultia in the Darling Range. He toyed with the idea of acquiring a piece of land in the Darling Range and the opportunity to do so arose eventually. A man came to him for financial advice at one stage and it turned out that he owned sixty acres (24.3 hectares) of bush at Paull's Valley, north of Kalamunda, in the hills close to Mundaring Weir. It had been taken up by a timberman in the 1930s and was almost totally undeveloped.

Paul bought the block for two hundred and fifty pounds, sight unseen. For the rest of his life, this piece of land, with a fine view over the

Helena River, the Swan Valley and the city of Perth in the distance, would serve him as a refuge from the rigours of public life. But in these early years, while Rollo and I were still at Prac, it was a place we went to on weekends in order to create a rough bush track through the jarrah and banksia trees to the edge of the escarpment. We worked hard on that track and when we finally brought it close to the edge, we helped Paul build a corrugated-iron shed to house a couple of beds and an array of spades and mattocks and other tools. Rollo and I and our various friends camped on this bush block many times as the years went by, exploring caves on the property or hiking to the weir.

Towards the end of our time at Prac School, that phase of our life began to change. In late 1949, my father was elected to the federal parliament in Canberra as a Liberal Party member for the newly created seat of Curtin. This encompassed the suburbs surrounding Freshwater Bay, and suburbs further afield such as Subiaco, Wembley and West Leederville.

Rollo and I played a part in his election by joining campaign workers in stuffing pamphlets in letter boxes in various parts of the electorate, me on one side of the street, Rollo on the other. In those days, politicians used to stand on street corners (usually on the back of a truck or a ute) and use a speaker hooked up to the power line overhead to broadcast their views to those in the vicinity. So we heard a few speeches (often more or less the same speech) as we moved around with our pamphlets. All of these tactics were put to use again in the double dissolution election of 1951 held eighteen months later.

After this second election, there was a round of speculation as to whether Paul Hasluck would be appointed to the front bench of the Menzies government. I will turn to my father's book *A Time for Building* for his account of what happened. He began by saying that after polling day on 28 April 1951, when more than a week had gone by, he assumed that he had been passed over again, so in the second week of May he went off to some rented rooms at Augusta in the south west of the state with his wife Alix and two small sons for a holiday. Paul continued in this way,

On the evening of 9 May, when we returned all wet and sandy with a sugar bag of fish, Mrs Styles, the landlady at the little pub at Augusta, told me: 'Someone has been trying to get you urgently on the telephone and the post-mistress knows all about it.'

My first thought was of family illness or fatality. The elderly postmistress, who lived and worked in a little cottage down the road, could only say that it was 'someone from Brisbane' who wanted me urgently. In those days telephone communication with Augusta closed at 5 p.m. but arrangements had been made to re-open the line at 8 o'clock. When the call came through to the hotel about 8.30 p.m. it turned out to be the private secretary of Menzies calling from a Brisbane Hotel.

I took the call at a telephone hanging on the wall of a passage way in the Augusta hotel. It was one of those old-fashioned instruments with a handle to whirl when you took a call and when you ended it. Presently Menzies came on the line. He asked me where I was. He asked me if I could get to Canberra. He wanted me to do a job for him but he couldn't say anything over the telephone. Then, apologising because he had to return to dinner guests, he handed the phone back to his private secretary and we worked out some travel plans.

Paul said of the family holiday at Augusta, a short break cut even shorter by the call from Brisbane that led to his appointment as Minister for Territories, and to a further appointment in due course as Minister for External Affairs, that it was 'the last organised holiday I attempted to have for the next 18 years. It had lasted 2 days.'

This untimely end to family holidays came about because his commitments in the first portfolio took him not only to parliamentary sittings in Canberra but also to remote regions in Papua and New Guinea and the Northern Territory. His work as Foreign Minister in the 1960s was equally demanding because the pressure of world events kept him constantly occupied, including periods of travel to South East Asia, London and New York. One can't help wondering what effect a frequently absent father had on Rollo during his formative years and early adult life.

In the years after the phone call from Menzies, my parents were never able to find the time to go on family picnics or similar outings. There were, however, some compensatory events. Soon after Paul's appointment, we made an excursion that included some unusual adventures and proved to be a memorable experience for Rollo and me.

The Territories portfolio included the administration of Norfolk Island, so the Hasluck family was able to spend a few weeks on that seductive fragment of the South Pacific while my father attended to some official business. We were to stay at Government House, a lovely old Georgian building, solidly constructed of limestone with spacious, stone-flagged verandas. On the way to it from the island's tiny airport, we became aware of huge grey stone walls and gateways, tall buildings, some ruinous and roofless, others obviously still used. This avenue was called Quality Row, for here the garrison officers and their families had lived during convict days. Not far from Government House were the ruins of the main prison, and a place called Bloody Bridge, where the gang of convicts who were building it revolted against the cruelty of the warder, murdered him and built his body into the foundations of the bridge.

Norfolk Island is a beautiful place adorned with grassy fields and majestic Norfolk pine trees. The island is surrounded by seas of the deepest blue curving into little bays situated beneath towering cliffs, most of them rising steeply from the beaches and rocky outcrops below.

We were very comfortable in the official residence, looked after by a pleasant housekeeper, for the island was between administrators for a couple of weeks. We walked and swam and visited the convict ruins. It was there, while riding with Paul and Rollo, that I came close to being dashed to death on jagged rocks. My horse bolted, then came to sudden halt at a cliff's edge, affording me a frightening glimpse of the sea-splashed rocks below. I was riding a feisty former racehorse, I was told later. I wish I had been told that before we set out.

Most of what we were told about the island came from the housekeeper or from local residents such as members of the Buffett family. They were descendants of the *Bounty* mutineers who had moved from Pitcairn Island – the mutineers' first place of refuge – to the more favourable conditions on Norfolk Island, further to the south, above New Zealand. Peter

Buffett was about Rollo's age and soon became our particular friend. On bike or by horseback, he took us to every corner of the island and showed us some of his secret hiding-places. One of them was behind a massive heap of empty, cobwebbed beer bottles at the rear of a decaying mansion on Quality Row, the broad avenue where the first settlement was established.

It was too expensive to ship the empties back to Australia, Peter explained, as we stared at the heap, so the pile of brown bottles had steadily expanded, year by year. It was now much admired by members of his family circle: an ivy-shrouded monument to conviviality over many decades, a miscellany of glass containers raised to beer and skittles in other days.

Upon returning to Perth, we resumed our normal round, which still included going to the Windsor Theatre and other cinemas for Saturday afternoon matinees. It wasn't long after our return that we were fortunate enough to see a version of *Mutiny on the Bounty* starring Charles Laughton as Captain Bligh and Clark Gable as the mutineer Fletcher Christian. This was not the only movie drawn from history. There were films based on Robin Hood and Captain Kidd, and John Mills starred in a movie about Scott of the Antarctic. There was no shortage of westerns starring John Wayne, Gary Cooper and Randolph Scott. The Olympic star Johnny Weismuller was often seen as Tarzan or Jungle Jim.

Some years later, I did my best to recapture the thrill of it all by writing a poem called 'Matinees', a satirical piece of which, I am pleased to say, Rollo thoroughly approved.

> I saw Weissmuller in my time
> run antelopes to earth
> and wrestle in the shallows
> of a film director's mind – killing
> the crocodiles single-handed.
>
> Knowing what to expect
> that was the beauty of it –
> the iron-clad figure crumpling

on the battlements, a hand
pressed to his side as if seized
by indigestion, the crossbow
falling from him as he fell,
always hit the water.

The serials never ended –
up to his neck in quicksand,
the hero, six days later,
was only buried to the knee
and his shirt had dried out;
he grasped the trailing vine;
the tarantulas, out of courtesy,
had fallen back a foot or two
and the deadly piranha fish,
this week, weren't biting.

These were stagecoach days
when the breech was never empty
and judgement, riding shotgun,
fell sideways to the first arrow –
matinees, afternoons like covered
wagons formed in tight circles
against the marauding world…

The cavalry rides backwards
into the hills and waits there
for the slow hand-clap;
time is counted out; the screen
spills dwindling numbers
into darkness.

Another School

The usual practice at that time was for students to move on to a secondary school in the year they turned thirteen years of age. This meant, if they stayed the distance, and if things ran smoothly, that they would sit for the junior certificate in the year they turned fifteen and for the leaving certificate two years later when they turned seventeen.

It seems that in the course of 1951, when Rollo was ten years of age, the Hasluck parents, Paul and Alix, formed a view that Rollo, who was thought to be one of the bright boys in his class at Prac, was not being fully extended. They looked around and came to the conclusion that their sons would be better off at Scotch College, a Presbyterian private school in the nearby suburb of Swanbourne. Some improvement in my father's financial circumstances, as a result of becoming a cabinet minister, may also have played a part in their thinking. They could meet the fees charged by a private school.

The outcome of these deliberations was that at the beginning of 1952 Rollo and I were enrolled at Scotch College. In that era, the allocation of a class level was determined by reference to one's birthday in the calendar year. Born in January 1941, Rollo, in the usual case, would have joined a primary school class at Scotch consisting of others born in that year. It seems, however, that his parents arranged for him to skip a class with the result that he entered the senior school at Scotch College earlier than usual and eventually sat for the junior certificate in the year he turned fourteen years of age.

It came about, then, that in all the years of his secondary schooling Rollo was younger than most of those in his class. He had been only one year ahead of me at Prac School, but at Scotch College he was now notionally two years ahead of me. Unlike the situation at Prac where we were both part of the same group, he quickly acquired his own set of friends, and they were mostly older than he was. He had a good physique and matured early. In the years that followed, he was generally able to pass for older than his actual age.

He was keen to keep up with his generally older friends and, in doing so, probably keen to impress them. I am inclined to think, looking back on it all, that he increasingly gave more weight to doing well at sport and in socialising than in doing well in class. This was probably not what my parents had in mind when he was moved to a higher class at another school, but the decision had been made, and the die was cast.

Scotch College had been set up in 1897. By the early 1950s, under the leadership of the headmaster at that time, Maxwell Keys, it was on a sound footing and its plans for the future were suitably ambitious. Various improvements to the fabric of the so-called College on the Hill were carried into effect in that era including the construction of a Memorial Hall on the main campus and the completion of the Gooch Pavilion overlooking the school playing fields adjacent to what was known then as Butler's Swamp, but now as Lake Claremont.

Maxwell Keys sought to appoint well-qualified teachers from the eastern states, New Zealand or England and many of them were at the school for many years. Their ranks included the deputy headmaster Alfred Jenkinson, Don Thomas, 'Dang' Gardiner, Willliam Dancer, Patrick 'Jumbo' McGushin, Joan Secombe, Ray 'Mick' Gamble, Jim Mathers and the well-known West Australian writer, Peter 'Mo' Cowan. Sporting teams had access to well-qualified part-time coaches such as Mervyn Inverarity for cricket and Austin Robertson for athletics and football. Both of them had sons at the school who were destined to achieve fame in later life: John Inverarity as a test cricketer and Austin Robertson junior as a champion at Subiaco Football Club and the state's leading goal kicker for many seasons.

There were four 'houses' at Scotch College at that time: School House, Cameron, Stewart and St Andrews. Rollo and I, and a number of other newcomers, were assigned to St Andrews and quickly became accustomed to marching into the area set aside for school assemblies to the sound of bagpipes, for a pipe band, arrayed in tartan kilts, white shirts and black caps, was a long-standing tradition at the school.

Rollo's classmates in the years that followed included some friends from Prac such as Ken Freeman and Colin Mayrhofer, and new friends, mostly from the surrounding suburbs, such as John Rigg, Jim Lang, Roger Dawkins, Gavin Bunning and many others. His closest friends came from a group of talented swimmers, most of whom, again, were older than he was. Some of these were friends known to him already from the baths and from Claremont Swimming Club. They were lively and likeable characters, his swimming mates, a number with colourful nicknames: Geoff 'Egg' Eastaugh, John 'Nons' Nelson, Rod 'Ogger' Newman, Peter Halliday, and the two brothers Tim and Jerry Knowles.

Rollo excelled in swimming while at Scotch, in the inter-house competition and as a member of the Scotch team at the inter-school sports held at Crawley Baths, close to Matilda Bay in Nedlands. In his final year at Scotch, he combined with Halliday, Nelson and Easthaugh to win the open medley relay event. But Scotch was not the only place to excel. Throughout the summer months, he entered races held by the Claremont Swimming Club on Tuesday nights. He soon made a name for himself at the club as an outstanding competitor, especially in breast stroke. On one occasion, at the State Swimming Championships, he won the under-fifteen years breaststroke event in record time.

Swimming was by no means the only sport of interest to us. Rollo and I had followed the fortunes of the Australian cricket team led by Lindsay Hassett that went to England in 1953 but lost the Ashes. We were thrilled to see the rivals in action when the English team, captained by Len Hutton, came to Australia a year later, although, as will become apparent from the story I am about to tell – a story destined to become part of our family folklore – our thrill was upended to some extent by my mother's sardonic indifference to how important the Ashes were.

Our chance to see the visiting cricket team came about in this way.

We were still living at 2 Adams Road, riding our bikes to Scotch on weekdays, but when school holidays arrived, we sometimes flew to the east coast for a family get together in Canberra, or perhaps Sydney, or even further afield, as in the case of our excursion to Norfolk Island. In December 1954, on one of these trips, we finished up staying with our parents at Ushers Hotel, Castlereagh Street, in the centre of Sydney. In its fight to retrieve the Ashes, Australia had won the first test match in Brisbane and the second test was now under way at the Sydney Cricket Ground. To our great delight it turned out that Paul had got hold of some tickets to the last few days.

We sat with him in the stand as play proceeded. England was out for 154 in its first innings, a score exceeded by the Australians with 228 runs. We were then treated to a marvellous display of batting by Bill Edrich, Colin Cowdrey and Peter May in the course of the visiting team's second innings, with May reaching 104 before Ray Lindwall took his wicket shortly before lunch on the fourth day. The Australian team began their second innings mid-afternoon, needing 233 runs to win, and thus the scene was set for an exciting finish on the final day.

That evening, Paul and Alix took us to a small Chinese restaurant near the hotel, and that too was exciting because (Australia being what it was in the 1950s) Rollo and I had never eaten Chinese food before. A trio of musicians under Chinese lanterns in a corner of the basement venue kept us entertained as the three males at the table weighed up the prospects of an Australian victory and did our best to explain to Alix what was at stake. This was difficult because she didn't have the slightest interest in sport of any kind, and to hear it being said that the English fast bowler Frank 'Typhoon' Tyson had apparently increased his pace, and his accuracy, by reverting to a shorter run-up, and now looked to be a real threat, as evidenced by the wickets he had taken already – those of Les Favell and Jim Burke – simply prompted Alix to suggest that it was about time we changed the subject.

Next morning, to Alix's absolute horror, it turned out that at short notice my father had to attend an important meeting, with the result that

Alix would have to look after the two boys by taking them to the cricket ground. She protested, but to no avail, and off we went. She had armed herself with an Agatha Christie novel and this she began reading soon after play started, looking up occasionally if she heard a round of applause.

According to Paul, as he always told the story in later years, he finally managed to get to the ground later in the day, conscious, as he shouldered his way towards the grandstand, that the crowd seemed to be swelling, possibly in response to news on the radio as to what was taking place on the field.

He slipped into a seat beside his wife and quickly whispered, 'What's happening?'

She had finished her Agatha Christie by now and was inclined to speak freely. 'Nothing!' she said. 'This is the most boring day I've spent in my entire life.' She gestured at the players below. 'They keep ambling about, but they don't seem to be doing anything in particular.'

When Paul turned to his eldest son, he was presented with an entirely different picture. It was one of the best days' cricket he had ever seen, Rollo said. Australia had begun the last day needing 151 runs to win, but Typhoon Tyson, by sheer pace, had cut a swath through the Australian side. Neil Harvey had batted heroically as the Australian wickets fell around him – Hole, Benaud, Archer, Davidson, Lindwall, Langley – and now it was down to Harvey and the tail-ender Bill Johnston, with Australia still requiring 46 runs to win!

Paul was there when the end came. Johnston nicked a ball from Tyson. The English wicketkeeper, Godfrey Evans, took the catch. The game was over, leaving Neil Harvey 92 not out, having played one of the finest innings of his career. England had won the match by 38 runs. Tyson had become only the third fast bowler ever to take 10 wickets in a test match for England against Australia. The commentators claimed that this was one of the most exciting finishes to have taken place at the Sydney Cricket Ground for many years.

Needless to say, Alix was unmoved by these statistics. She felt a little better that evening, once we got back to the hotel, when she found that we would be going to see a Gilbert and Sullivan production the following night. I was somehow left with an impression from all of this, with the benefit of adult hindsight admittedly, that after her day at the Sydney Cricket Ground, Alix always thought of cricket, with its chorus lines of flannelled players coming and going, all in white, one or two with coloured caps on their heads, as some sort of peculiar comic opera, but far too long and without a plot.

Scotch College put on theatrical productions of course, under the direction of the French teacher, Miss Joan Secombe, but, as far as I am aware, Rollo was never recruited to play a part. He was, however, involved in dressing up of another kind.

Like a good many of his friends and classmates at Scotch, Rollo joined the school cadet corps. They all went off to the army camp at Northam, sixty miles to the east of Perth, on several occasions. For formal parades, his uniform, like the others, consisted of a tartan kilt, khaki jacket and beret. He was with the same crowd when they began going to parties with girls from the neighbouring schools, such as Scotch's so-called 'sister' school, Presbyterian Ladies College, or St Hilda's, the Anglican school. There were dances also at the Dalkeith Hall, the Claremont Football Club and the King's Park Tennis Club.

Rollo's first attraction to the social scene began slightly before the rock 'n' roll era initiated by Bill Haley and Elvis Presley. He and his mates were initially beguiled by jazz or whatever was on the hit parade. I can remember Rollo bringing home his first 78rpm record: *When The Saints Go Marching In*, played by Graham Bell's Australian jazz band, a group that had toured Europe in the 1940s. That first record was quickly followed by Louis Armstrong's *Basin Street Blues*, and later by some more dixieland jazz. The pile of black shellac 78 rpm records mounted. Glen Miller and Benny Goodman were greeted with approval, as were Dizzy Gillespie and Stan Getz. Rollo's first 33 rpm records included *Crazy Hamp* by Lionel Hampton and *Perdido* by the Buddy de Franco trio. Then rock 'n' roll and jiving began to make their presence felt. It was at this time that Rollo began going off to dances in tight trousers and a baggy green jumper called a sloppy joe.

More than once, according to the custom in those days, I went into the city with Rollo and one or two of his mates – cast in the role of 'younger brother tagging along' – to see what was happening in the record shops and to find out what had just come in. We would all cram into a booth at the store to check the quality of a proposed purchase, sometimes with headphones on, sometimes not, depending on the particular store. The radiograms of families in the neighbourhood gradually got larger and sleeker.

On the home front, at 2 Adams Road, Rollo and I were also keeping up with other cultural trends. Our father was constantly away at parliamentary sittings in Canberra or on visits to far places. He was joined by Alix from time to time for official occasions involving the Minister for Territories. This meant that arrangements had to be made for the boys. So my parents usually engaged a live-in housekeeper called Mrs Hammer to keep things going.

Mrs Hammer was a short, stout middle-aged lady with a no-nonsense manner. She did everything that was expected of her, and did it well. In the evening, after dinner, she liked to sit at a bridge table set up in the middle of the lounge room where she would play cards – mostly patience – and listen to the radio. Occasionally, when she was joined by a friend, Rollo and I would be recruited to make up a foursome. We spent many hours in that way listening to the quiz shows conducted by the giants of Australian radio: Bob Dyer and Jack Davey, feisty media personalities, overflowing with quips and good-humoured backchat, but personalities scarcely known to my parents.

Rollo and I had grown up with *Dick Barton (Special Agent)*, and the BBC's comedy show *Much Binding in the Marsh*, but we soon became devotees of the quiz shows. The merits of Dyer and Davey, and the nature of their rivalry on air, were matters of real interest to Mrs Hammer and her closest friend. On the whole, they seemed to prefer Bob Dyer, and the Palmolive products he recommended, although his American background weighed against him to some extent. We listened mostly to *Pick-*

a-Box, where Dyer's contestants were eventually faced with an agonising question: the money or the box? Should one take the money won so far or pick the box that could be worth much more? Mrs Hammer usually opted for the bird in the hand, and was quietly pleased if a box was picked and turned out disappointing. 'That'll teach him,' she would say, as the ever-cheerful Bob Dyer farewelled the contestant to a round of applause.

Maybe it was the jazz, or perhaps the socialising. One way or another, Rollo and his confederates at school, or from around the neighbourhood, found their way to smoking cigarettes in quiet haunts. Dances at the King's Park Tennis Club or other places some distance away sometimes led to surreptitious joy rides in family vehicles commandeered by older members of the group (a pastime generally called 'thrashing the wagon').

Some of the swimmers, including Rollo, were sporting crew cuts or styling their hair in the so-called Kramer cut, named after the famous American tennis star Jack Kramer. This consisted of long sideburns with a plateau of closely shaved hair on top. It didn't take long for this peculiar look to be strictly forbidden by the Scotch authorities. Rollo and several of his friends challenged this puritanical edict, on the grounds that the cut in question, provided by a legendary hairdresser in the city, Sam Rifici, helped them swim faster by reducing the water resistance. Their case was prejudiced by reports from parents and masters about their smoking: the 'fast' lives they were leading.

Things came to a head at about the time Rollo was sitting exams for the junior certificate. I wasn't privy to exactly what happened, but I was left with a general impression that, for various reasons, which probably included being caught smoking and refusing to modify his haircut, the headmaster told my parents that, in his opinion, Rollo would probably do better at another school. My belief is that the matter didn't quite reach the point of expulsion because my parents were of the same opinion. Things didn't seem to be working out for Rollo at Scotch College and there were no signs that the situation would improve.

Rollo scraped through his exams but, by the end of the school year, as a consequence of the deliberations about his future, it was resolved that at the commencement of the next school year he would be enrolled as a boarder at Canberra Grammar School. By now, the pressures of ministerial work meant that Paul was spending most of his time out of Perth, because travel back and forth in those days, even by air, took so long. He had a small flat near Canberra Grammar School, so the idea was that he would be able to keep a closer eye on Rollo's progress by taking him out of the boarding house from time to time, usually on weekends.

But all of this lay in the future. For Rollo, accustomed to living in the moment, the forthcoming summer in Perth was the main thing. He went sailing at Rockingham and on the river by the Claremont and Freshwater Bay yacht clubs, in clinker-built cadet dinghies or in the sleeker and faster sharpies. He spent several weeks at Rottnest with a group of friends, in a cottage overlooking the beach at Thomson Bay.

Some years later, I wrote a poem in which I sought to capture the charm of Rottnest at that time for those who began going there in the summer months from their earliest days at school, with parents or with their mates, and for many years thereafter.

> All day the bicycles come and go
> from General Store to bungalow.
>
> From bungalow to Bakery and back
> to get the makings of a midday snack.
>
> At night, again, like carefree ships,
> the bikes drift past on random trips.
>
> Down to the Tearooms beneath the stars,
> a younger brother on the handlebars.
>
> To visit the pub; friends, perhaps,
> jokes about fishing, afternoon naps.
>
> A hand of cards and a quiet beer.
> the days cycle past, year by year.
>
> Cycling back to the bungalow,
> we can see the mainland lights aglow.

> Out there, way out, that luminous shelf,
> the haze of light and the city itself.

In February 1956, Rollo set off for his new school. I stayed on at Scotch College, living at home with my mother. She was, by this time, writing the first of her various books, *Portrait with Background,* about one of the early West Australian settlers, Georgiana Molloy, an amateur botanist who became well-known eventually for the samples she collected while living at Augusta in the south-west of the state and which were then sent to Kew Gardens in London for study and safekeeping.

I visited Canberra from time to time with my parents but, in describing the next two years of Rollo's life, I am largely dependent on his letters home, bits and pieces in the Canberra Grammar School magazine, and tales told in my presence by his friends and classmates.

Canberra Days

When the foundation stone of Canberra Grammar School was laid in December 1928, it was assumed that the new academy would develop as a boarding school catering mainly for boys coming from the Anglican Diocese of Goulburn. Canberra was the national capital, true, but at that time there were few signs that it was destined to become a major city. Buildings were dotted about the landscape like punctuation marks on a blank page. The fledgling school on Flinders Way, lying between the cluster of shops at Manuka and a scattering of residential dwellings at the foot of Red Hill in Deakin, was surrounded by bushland, with some farming properties in the distance.

The school, like Canberra itself, gradually expanded. The appointment of Canon Garnsey in 1948 led to an increase in the number of students, but progress was slow. It appears from the recollections of the Reverend 'Jack' Tyrell, who joined the school's teaching staff in 1952, that the school in that year had 123 boarders and 83 day boys. He added, 'It is a very small school made up almost entirely of country boys. Its future is very much in the balance as it is heavily in debt.'

Tyrell's account of the facilities was equally dour.

> Entering the quadrangle, there was indeed a completed wing on the left which I later found had classrooms at the bottom and dormitories above. Immediately in front of the viewer was an imposing dining hall under which there were two laboratories and a small library. To the right was an isolated unfinished block called Garran House for a group of very small boys. What is now the front of the school was completely vacant, giving a fine view over the oval and the distant Canberra. I discovered later that there were other less distinguished buildings tucked away all over the grounds, most of

them old army huts. Of them, the chapel was the most interesting. The quad was a dirt playground for one and all, very dusty in dry weather and a quagmire in wet.

At the time of Rollo's arrival in February 1956, the school was a little larger but not much had changed. He was allotted a bed in one of the dormitories above the classrooms in the completed wing and, along with other newcomers, was given some instructions by the housemaster, Roy Morrow, about mundane matters such as making one's bed in the morning and lining up for meals in the dining hall. The newcomer from Perth soon discovered that the boilers somewhere out the back, in the vicinity of the dining hall, which were meant to be underpinning the hot water system, were often on the blink. A cold shower on a cold Canberra morning may have been character building but, on the whole, it wasn't amusing.

Rollo's dormitory overlooked a small apple orchard attached to the headmaster's house situated to one side of the main establishment. Rollo was always quick to make new friends and soon learnt that raids on the headmaster's orchard after dark were quite common. One of his early letters revealed that he had acquired the nickname 'Wally'. We on the home front assumed this came from a mispronunciation of his name Rollo. Not so. It seems that when he and his mates were apprehended by the gardener in the course of an orchard raid, he gave his name as Wally Donovan – echoing the name of the skiffle group king of that era, Lonnie Donegan. Rollo was known by his fellow boarders thereafter as Wally or Wal.

Rollo quickly proved himself as a swimmer. The school had three houses at that time: Blaxland, Sheaffe and Jones. Rollo was assigned to Jones House and did well for his house at the inter-house swimming carnival. Having turned fifteen years of age in January, shortly before the school term started, he could swim for Jones in both the under age and open categories. He won not only the under-sixteen breaststroke and butterfly races but also, over 110 yards, the open freestyle and breaststroke events, plus, over 55 yards, the open butterfly. When I analyse the results presented in the school magazine for 1956, it strikes me that he should have been awarded the Bracegirdle Cup for the best overall performance, but for whatever reason it was in fact awarded to his friend Michael Snow. At the inter-school carnival soon afterwards, he won the butterfly race over 55 yards in both the open and under-sixteen categories.

He had played only Australian rules football in Perth but it seems he quickly adapted to rugby union and was given a place in the CGS 1st XV. A photo of the team in the school magazine shows him with many of those who were by now his friends at the school: Arthur Roberts, Phil Nadin, Dave Brown, Tony May, David Julien, Gerald Focken, Tony Hewitt and Claude Hargreaves. The team came second to Canberra High School in the inter-school competition but is said to have been overwhelmed by the Catholic contingent from St Patrick's College at Goulburn.

Rollo lined up with some other friends in the school play – *The Tempest* – being cast as Gonzalo, 'an honest old counsellor'. In a letter home he said, 'We have our first dress rehearsal of *The Tempest* tonight. It should be fun. I've got to have a great long beard and I've had to let my hair grow all this term so it is just about down over my shoulders.' A friend of Rollo's from Tumbarumba, George Martin, was cast as the 'savage and deformed slave Caliban'. A friend from Canberra, Peter May – one of the day boys – played an attendant lord.

A review in the school magazine began by noting that this isn't one of Shakespeare's best plays but the cast 'tackled it well.' The review added, 'Martin, in particular, revelled in the wallowing of the earthy Caliban, scaring little boys in the front seats… Hargreaves as Ferdinand, Hasluck as Gonzalo, and Brown in the very difficult part of Alonso, did justice to three rather colourless characters.'

The fearsome George Martin reappeared in the house debates, as did Rollo and others from the school play. On one topic – whether there was too much sport in Australia – 'Martin exhausted the subject, and neither Brown, with his dismal tale of the hard-walking golfers, nor Oldfield, could say very much more. Ross shone for Jones, as did also Hasluck, who, having little more than Brown or Oldfield to say, nevertheless said it fluently and entertainingly.'

When it came to a debate against the neighbouring Church of England Girls School as to whether 'we should sever our link with England', Martin led the CGS team, followed by Brown and Hasluck. The tenor of the proceedings was set from the moment the boys marched in carrying the Union Jack and singing 'Rule Britannia'. It seems that having had the house debates for practice, the boys were able to talk about nothing and get away with it. The girls, as usual, talked a lot of sound sense, according to the adjudicator, the Reverend Jack Tyrell, but in the end they couldn't cope with the boys' practised debating skills.

Rollo was back in Perth for Christmas and the summer vacation. He quickly renewed his relationship with friends in the neighbourhood and at Claremont Baths, especially those from the Scotch swimming team in other days such as Nons Nelson, Egg Eastaugh, Ogger Newman, Peter Halliday and a good many others. There was also fishing, crabbing and sailing to be done. This was mostly centred on the northern end of Freshwater Bay, but with occasional excursions to Point Walter and Blackwall Reach, where the river turned towards Fremantle on its way to the Indian Ocean.

Well rested, Rollo returned to Canberra Grammar early in 1957, now aged sixteen. He was all set for more sport and the run-up to the end-of-year exams – a chance to obtain his leaving certificate and matriculate. This proved to be a very crowded year. His friend Arthur Roberts was appointed school captain, a number of his other friends were named as prefects and he himself became a sub-prefect.

It appears from the school magazine that for the third year in succession, CGS won the inter-school swimming competition. In the annual carnival held at the Olympic pool in Canberra, seventeen records were shattered, of which Rollo broke four. He played a leading role in the house debates and in the Jones versus Blaxland contest was described as one of the best debaters of the night. Later in the year, in place of a cancelled debate against St Edmund's, a panel including Rollo and George

Martin 'gave a good account of themselves and were not afraid to give their honest opinions on even the most controversial issues'. In the debate against the girl's school, 'Miss McLennan and Hasluck both "whipped" well, but Miss McLennan was the more fiery and effective of the two.'

Girls were now well and truly on the agenda of Rollo and his brown-suited classmates, via the ballroom dancing class. These occasional get-togethers with the girls' school were described by one participant (somewhat sarcastically) as follows:

> A glittering assembly – 20 sartorial brown uniforms on the right, 20 immaculate green uniforms on the left. On the right, 20 eager faces, with expressions showing confidence and poise; on the left, 20 smiles as charming as they are modest, and in the centre, Madam and Sir, equipped of course with their standard tools of trade (heavy duty boots with metal toe caps). All are hushed expectantly. And then it happens! Loudly the voice of the immortal bard, Danny Kaye, beats down upon our ears…

These supposedly glittering assemblies led eventually to a dance in the school hall 'made possible by the presence of girls from Canberra High School as well as our old friends from the girls' school'. This was followed a little later by the excitement of a dance at the girls' school shortly before the year ended. Perhaps this is why Rollo satisfied the examiners in only three subjects – English, French and Geography – and thus, having failed to obtain the New South Wales leaving certificate at his first attempt, was destined to return to CGS the following year for another shot at it.

My parents then decided that I should join Rollo as a boarder at Canberra Grammar School. Rollo turned seventeen a month or so before the school year started and quickly obtained his driving licence. While we were staying in my father's flat at 60 Macgregor Street, Deakin, quite close to the school, Rollo was often at the wheel of the family Peugeot as the final weeks of the summer holiday ran out. Firearms could be easily acquired in those days and, as it happened, my father had a couple of shot guns and a .22 rifle. He took us on shooting trips from time to time on hills and ridges near the Murrumbidgee River, where we shot rabbits and foxes. Rollo and I would sometimes drive across to Queanbeyan to join his friend Bill Swan, son of a local businessman, on duck-shooting sorties.

Under Rollo's tuition, while opening and closing gates on dusty tracks, I became adept at boarding the old green Peugeot as it moved away, with Rollo or his friend at the wheel. As the departing car picked up speed, the gate-opener, like a bank robber scrambling into a getaway car, was expected to get a grip on the back door (held ajar by the passenger in the front seat) and haul himself into the back seat before the car's increasing momentum left him stranded in its dust.

Rollo had created this technique with another of his shooting mates, Peter 'Hooks' Ewens, son of the parliamentary draughtsman. My father, as the man who now felt obliged to lend his treasured Peugeot to his recently licensed elder son, would have been appalled if he had witnessed these getaway car scenes, like footage from a Keystone Cops movie, but fortunately he neither saw nor heard of what went on in his absence. I will come to the eventual fate of his precious Peugeot a little later.

A few days before term started, Rollo drove me up to the school for a glimpse of what lay ahead. A list on a noticeboard in the cloisters set out the names of those who were to serve as prefects and sub-prefects in the coming year. Rollo, who had previously been a sub-prefect, wasn't on the list. He was pondering this when a couple of his friends from the previous year turned up to collect some belongings. They had left the school by now, and had driving licences too, but were pleased indeed to have chanced upon their old mate. So arrangements were quickly made to rendezvous in a more convenient place. Within a few minutes, our car and three or four others had zoomed into the shade offered by the cluster of pine trees that used to stand at the Red Hill end of Melbourne Avenue, a stone's throw from the girls' school.

Rollo produced a packet of cigarettes and his offer was quickly accepted by the five or six of us in the group. He showed his friends our shotguns and the .22 rifle and they were duly impressed. Tales were told of summer adventures and of the deeds and misdeeds of others known to them all. Then, by chance, the chit-chat turned to the list on the school noticeboard and the strange omission of Rollo's name. Someone in the group surmised that the reason was possibly because Rollo was about to be named school captain! Ever the optimist, Rollo saw this as a real possibility, and said so. He was pleased to hear others affirming his opinion.

I wasn't quite so optimistic. These were early days, and I didn't yet know how things were done at this particular school. But if it was anything like Scotch College in Perth, I didn't rate Rollo's chances highly. There we were, beneath a pall of cigarette smoke, guns on the bonnet of our car like a wild bunch in a B-grade western, while Rollo, fag in hand, talked up his prospects. School captain? I didn't think so. He had been forced out of Scotch after an ill-advised flirtation with narcotics and here he was, toying with fate again. But I let the conversation run on because we were all having such a good time.

It struck me later, with the benefit of hindsight, that Rollo's name had probably been left off the list by mistake. He was one of those who had sat for the leaving certificate the previous year. Someone in the front office may have inadvertently assumed he wouldn't be coming back to the school.

But Rollo was like that. He generally looked on the bright side of things. He was good-hearted and always enjoyed the company of his friends. He was inclined to act impulsively, true, but this was often to his credit.

On one occasion, for example, in the course of these pre-term weeks, while my mother was briefly in Canberra, Rollo and I and a couple of his friends booked the CGS tennis courts – in those days dusty clay courts surrounded on all sides by high chicken-wire fences. Having dropped us off, my mother went on to Manuka to do some shopping. Upon her return journey, driving along Flinders Way towards Red Hill, she slowed down to toot the horn and give us a wave. Her moment of inattention meant that she misjudged the curve and ran off the road, finishing up in the undergrowth between the courts and the bitumen. Within seconds,

Rollo was scrambling up the chicken wire, an almost impossible feat, and jumped down to the other side. He managed to reach her right away.

Fortunately, she was unhurt. When the rest of us arrived – by a longer route through the nearest gate – we were able to push the car back on the road and watch her drive off safely. It was in Rollo's nature to act like that. Doing what had to be done, quick smart, and without concern for what it might cost, or for his bleeding hands.

Certainly, when I came to the school soon afterwards, Rollo did his best to settle me in without bloodshed or tears. In the weeks before term started, I had been doing fairly well at tennis, and had even managed to beat him at singles once or twice. Unbeknownst to me, Rollo spread the word in Jones House that I was a star. Within hours of my arrival, while I was upstairs in my dormitory, still unpacking (feeling rather miserable in fact), Ted Ussher, the school champion, arrived at my bedside. He had come straight from my brother and was still breathless after the run. Relieved to find I was available, he signed me up for the doubles.

In the weeks that followed, staggering under the burden he had been lumbered with, Ted Ussher carried us through to the finals and thence to victory. Sometimes, during the course of our partnership, watching my team mate speeding up and down the tramlines (on both sides of the court), I wondered what he thought of my brother. But no word of reproach ever crossed his lips.

Perhaps it was because Rollo was beyond reproach, being a veteran of last year's final year, something of an elder statesman. He was in his third year at the school. In addition to being captain of the school swimming team, he had participated in a good many feats of prowess. Being one of the few boys at the school with a driving licence was not the least of his achievements. The oversight that had led to his name being omitted from the list on the noticeboard had been rectified. He became a prefect, serving under Geoff Skein, whose name had been added to the list as school captain.

Another Shot

Rollo quickly recruited me to the Canberra Grammar swimming squad. In the first few weeks of the summer term, a group of us would get up early and trudge down to the Manuka Pool for training. We would find a patch of sunlight and sit there in our tracksuits for a while, shivering and staring soulfully at the water, before plunging in and thrashing up and down for half an hour or so.

In house competition, according to the CGS magazine, 'the best swimmers for Jones House were Hasluck R, and Hasluck N, winning the Open and Under 16 cups respectively'. In the main inter-school carnival in the open division, Rollo won the freestyle, and breaststroke races over 110 yards and the butterfly over 55 yards. I am pleased to recall, in looking at the magazine, that it includes two photos in which we are in the same groups, presented as team mates – brothers in the swimming team and the First XI cricket team. Rollo had excelled as a fast-bowler, inspired perhaps by having seen Typhoon Tyson in action.

Sport wasn't the only thing on our minds. From time to time, Roy Morrow, the housemaster, would let the boarders use the antiquated record player outside his office. On Saturday afternoons, if nothing else was happening, Rollo and some of his mates, with various younger hangers on like myself in tow, would lounge about in that vicinity listening to Bill Haley, Elvis Presley, Buddy Holly, Little Richard, Bo Diddley, the Big Bopper, and others of that era. 'Great Balls of Fire' by Jerry Lee Lewis was usually enough to bring the session to an end. 'That is more than enough,' the housemaster would say, bustling out of his office, pouting, turning off the machine with the air of a vigilante closing down a brothel.

For Rollo and me, brought up on Louis Armstrong's 'Basin Street

Blues' and Buddy de Franco's modernistic version of 'Perdido', jazz was still important. On Saturday nights, during term, there was often a film show in the gymnasium. After weeks of negotiation, Rollo, in his role as elder statesman, a veteran of the fifth form, a man who had sat for the leaving certificate last year and come close to escaping to the real world, managed to persuade the sports master, Vernon Davies, to get hold of *The Benny Goodman Story*.

A small group of enthusiasts saw the Goodman movie right through several times that weekend. Rollo, having virtually kidnapped the school projectionist, Spud Spedding, squeezed us all into the tiny projection room where we watched the jazz scenes on a makeshift screen about the size of an envelope. When Gene Krupa went wild on 'Sing, Sing, Sing', Rollo turned up the soundtrack until the drumbeat was deafening, a sudden threat to the gymnasts on the Roman rings below. Enraged by this, the sports master clambered up into our roost to find out what the hell was going on. 'Musical appreciation,' Rollo told him with aplomb. 'Don't get smart with me!' He turfed us out.

In the dormitories at night, there was sometimes music of another kind. The duty prefect was supposed to supervise the process of lights out. Rollo would sometimes appear in that role, clad in an off-white woollen jacket with a huge zip down the front. On other occasions, Alec Harris, an islander from Nauru, would often stroll into the dorm, wearing a tropical shirt, strumming a ukulele, crooning softly, to himself or to anyone amongst us who was prepared to listen.

By now, towards the end of the 1950s, the size and nature of Canberra Grammar School was beginning to change. There had been a large influx of day boys with parents in the public service or running local businesses. Students in the boarding house came mostly from the country towns near Canberra such as Goulburn, Yass, Cooma, Gundagai, Tarcutta, Tumbarumba, Tumut, and so on. But there were now also a few odd bods like ourselves – the sons of a parliamentarian – and some Asian students from diplomatic families, plus Alec Harris from Nauru.

Debating was still on the agenda, and for Rollo, it was of particular interest as a link to the girls' school at the far end of Mugga Way, beneath Red Hill. George Martin (formerly of Caliban fame), supported by Rollo and me, cast around for apt quotations and rode into the lists. As in all school debating, withering sarcasm was the order of the day. Rollo dished out more than his fair share of scorn. He would begin by saying that he intended to speak on the philosophical, historical, geographical, religious, economic, aesthetic, metaphysical, legal, governmental, medical and scientific aspects of the topic, while his brother (he would pause to lay a hand on my shoulder) would speak generally. The audience loved it. He flung vitriol around the room. They cheered.

The school magazine's coverage of these assaults on common sense was characteristically bland. It said,

> 1958 has been a most successful year for debating. There have been inter-school debates against St Patrick's, Royal Naval College, and the Girls' School. Martin and the Hasluck brothers have represented the School in these debates and won all but the Kitchen Trophy debate.

George Martin's exposure to the cut and thrust of debate at this time served him well. After leaving school. he was elected to the ACT Advisory Council and later, upon returning to his home town of Tumbarumba, served as mayor of the local municipality for many years.

The debate against the Royal Naval College came about in this way. For the first time, arrangements were made for Canberra Grammar to send its two senior rugby teams to play the naval cadets on the college ground at Jervis Bay on the south coast of New South Wales. Rollo was in the CGS First XV; I was in the Second XV. As we boarded the school bus, we didn't know what to expect. All sorts of rumours and forebodings were current. Rollo felt obliged to disclose that of the naval cadets, drawn from all quarters of the country, one was a West Australian who had run second to Herb Elliott at the inter-school sports in Perth. Worse, the naval cadets were said to have thrashed one of the Sydney teams, whipped Duntroon, devoured the local team at Nowra. They were animals. Things looked grim.

On the first morning of our visit, a bell sounded at a quarter to six. All the cadets tumbled out of bed and cantered on to the freezing parade ground in running shorts and singlets. They began exercising like fanatics – press-ups, sit-ups, knee-bends, running on the spot. Huddled in our blankets in the upper storey of the naval college, we stared at them in with a sense of awe and apprehension. We edged our way down to breakfast in a thoughtful frame of mind.

In the event, our First XV, which included Rollo and some of his rugged mates from the country towns, was able to beat the naval college by a narrow margin. My own team lost but went down bravely.

On the morning after the game, they took us out in a pair of crash boats. We found the ride exhilarating as the boats hammered up and down Jervis Bay at a great rate of knots, cornering and careering about the place in cascades of spray. It was sheer heaven.

We debated the cadets in the evening. We were able to see the cadets taking part in a full-dress parade on the Sunday morning. This was followed by a church parade and related service, which we all attended. We drove back to the school that afternoon, taking a tortuous route across the mountains, singing raucously in the dark on the final leg of the journey – 'Banana Boat Song', 'This Old Man Came Rolling Home' and many others.

Communal singing brings me to another facet of Rollo's life at Canberra Grammar. On Sundays, most of the boarders were expected to attend two services in the small chapel at the back of the school, one of the former army huts still situated in bushland, shaded by gum trees. Evensong at five-thirty included a sermon (by either the headmaster or the Reverend Jack Tyrell) and various well-known hymns, the lusty singing of which Rollo and I greatly enjoyed. There was also a mid-morning communion service. Boys from other denominations, or who weren't confirmed, were generally excused from this attendance. They were, instead, required to congregate in one of the classrooms and write dutiful letters home to their parents, under the watchful eye of a prefect.

Rollo and I were members of the letter-writing group – a small group in that era, for most of the boarders came from churchgoing Anglican families in country towns – and in my first year at Canberra Grammar Rollo was the prefect in charge. Or perhaps I should say supposedly in charge. After gathering his congregation together, Rollo would stand before us with upraised hands like Billy Graham and tell us to get on with it. Then, while he settled down to reading whatever was the current piece of hot literature, *Peyton Place* or some such, the rest of us would be left to chat amiably about sport or girls or whatever else was topical, scribbling a few paragraphs on our pads now and again if we ran out of things to say. Comics were exchanged and the occasional paper plane zigzagged through the air. Rollo's countercultural regime was quite blissful, and stood in stark contrast to the worshipful proceedings on the far side of the school campus

I see from some of the letters written by Rollo in his days at Canberra Grammar that he managed to send a few pages home, although most of them seem to have been written early on. The first letter in the bundle is dated 9 April 1956, soon after he started at the school.

> Dear Mum – we had the school fete on Saturday. I was on the 'Horse Rides' stall. It was good fun riding the horses to and from the stables but not so good leading them round with little kids on them… Over Easter Dad and I had a pretty good time shooting rabbits. We got six. We saw quite a few foxes but they were too far away to shoot. One fox we saw had a dead rabbit in its mouth. I am going out with Dad next Sunday.
>
> Next Sunday night about 6 of us Presbyterian boys at the school go to St Andrews, as we usually do once a month, and have a good time eating all the supper. The last time we went the Rev Harrison complimented me on your book saying what a fine piece of true history it was. This surprised the others a bit as they didn't know that I belonged to an authoress as well as an author (because Dad has books in the library). There isn't much more to say now, so I guess I'll close. Yours sincerely, Rollo.

The last letter in the bundle is dated 30 October 1958, by which time Rollo was in charge of the letter-writing group and getting close to sitting his final exams.

Dear Mum – I just received your letter this morning. Tentative arrangements stand as follows. Assuming you can, or Dad can, be over here by about 23rd or 24th Nov I can go to the Ewens on Sat 15th and stay there till Friday 21st, then 'bach' at MacGregor Street for a couple of days till you come over.

There is no need to panic at the thought of me batching. I'm a 'big boy' now – in case you didn't know. One thing is for certain – I can't stay at the school. Mr Morrow has told us that if we stay at the school we are to be treated as ordinary boys. This of course rules out any possibility of me (or anyone else in 5th year for that matter) staying at the school after the exams. That is just one of the reasons for me not staying. Another is that there is a big party at a girl's place on either the 15th or 22nd so I'll have to be out for that on account of the fact that I'm one of the V.I.Ps being farewelled at this party.

Regarding next year and my ideas, or 'desires' as you so tactfully put it. I think it might be better if I did get myself some qualifications first. As you say, short of going to Uni, accountancy seems about the best bet. I could do that for three years and then try that one year plan put out by Ford Motor Co which Dad sent me a pamphlet on.

Gee, it's been hot over here this week and the baths aren't opening till Sat. All of us are just burnt to a frazzle …. I've got a frantic haircut now. It's called a 'College Cut'. It's very short but not as short as a crewcut. Tell Dad that his gardens and lawns are looking well thanks to Nick and I. We both went down to Macgregor Street last Sunday afternoon and did a bit of work. At the moment I'm trying to study, but it's so hot that all I can think about is drinking and swimming. Well, I guess that's about it. Till I hear from you. Love, Rollo.

It emerges from this letter that Rollo's third and final year at Canberra Grammar was nearly over. The sport and good times were coming to an end. The time had come for Rollo to have another shot at the leaving certificate.

Paul and Alix seemed to assume that because Rollo had been through the examination process the previous year, and was repeating most of the subjects, he would sail through easily. But this was not to be. The good times had taken their toll. On this occasion, Rollo only managed to pass two subjects – English and General Mathematics. Nonetheless, according to the leaving certificate eventually issued to him, 'These results qualify the candidate for a pass in the Examination as a whole.' In other words, he was able to combine his passes in five subjects, achieved over two years, in order to obtain the certificate. It meant, however, that he hadn't matriculated and therefore didn't qualify for university entrance.

The time had come for Rollo to go back to Perth and look for a job, with or without the prospect of obtaining accountancy qualifications at night school in due course. There is, however, another facet of his schooldays in Canberra that should be mentioned before turning to his later life in the west. His various successes in local swimming carnivals led eventually to his participation in the annual country championship for New South Wales as a member of the team from ACT.

The best swimmers from country towns throughout the state were to meet at a carnival in Cessnock, north of Sydney. My father was keen to attend and managed to find the time to do so. We drove from Canberra to Cessnock in the course of a long day and checked in to a local pub in the main street. We found our way to the local pool right away, an arena swarming with tracksuited swimmers of all shapes and sizes, and established that Rollo's event – butterfly over 110 yards – was to take place early in the evening of the following day. I joined him in the crowded lanes of the pool for a few laps to loosen up, before heading back to the pub for a meal and a restful night.

I sat with my parents in the crowded stand throughout the next day. It was quickly apparent that the standard was high. The program revealed that one of the swimmers taking part was the Olympian Terry Gathercole from West Wylong. The afternoon faded into dusk and the arc lights around the turquoise pool were turned on.

Rollo and the other swimmers in his race trooped in, discarded their tracksuits, and lined up behind the starting blocks as their names were called. They mounted the blocks. They faced the floodlit pool. They waited for the starter's gun.

Rollo gave it all he had and was still with the leaders at the far end when they turned for the final lap. Perhaps he went out too fast. More likely, the swimmers in the central lanes were just too good. He finished seventh in a field of eight, his time a personal best, but we could see he was well and truly whacked. He could scarcely clamber out of the pool. He sat down abruptly on the nearest seat, chest heaving.

By the time I got down to the change rooms for a quick word he was all smiles, back to his usual self. 'That was some race!' he exclaimed, zipping up his tracksuit. 'That was really some race!' He seemed pleased it was all over. He had given it his best but the competition was too strong.

Rollo had packed a good deal into his Canberra days. He had made some close friends at the school, tried his hardest in all sorts of ways, from swimming to debating, and he had seen something of his father on weekends, when circumstances permitted. It emerges from Paul's book *The Chance of Politics,* in which he touches on these years, that the presence of his sons in Canberra worked out well. The arrangement, according to the author, led to benefits on both sides.

> I had the most appreciative tasters of my cooking that I have ever had. After a week or two of boarding house tucker the sort of dishes I gave them seemed like haute cuisine, and I must say my casserole of rabbit and my duckling with pickled walnuts were rather good for hungry boys in mid-winter. We had happy times.

The Early Sixties

Upon returning to Perth with a leaving certificate in his pocket, Rollo managed to pick up a desk job with the Yorkshire Insurance Company. Work as a clerk in the company's office in St Georges Terrace wasn't entirely to his liking, but one has to start somewhere, and it provided an income to support his weekend pursuits: mainly fishing and boating. His financial needs were modest as he was still living in the family home at 2 Adams Road.

I stayed on as a boarder at Canberra Grammar School during his first year back in the west, receiving occasional reports from home about his activities. At the beginning of 1960, having passed enough exams to get a leaving certificate and matriculate, I was back at 2 Adams Road myself, all set to embark upon a four-year law degree at the University of Western Australia. I saw little of Rollo in the first few months of my course because, while I was studying, he was socialising, dashing out to barbecues or parties hosted by local author Mary Durack, before going on to nightspots with her journalist daughter Patsy. Then, unexpectedly, on the Easter long weekend of that year, Rollo and I spent some memorable days together.

For some reason which is still not entirely clear to me, but possibly due to the need for a second car on the home front, my father decided to transfer his car in Canberra, the old green Peugeot, to Perth. The journey, according to his carefully thought out plan of action, was to begin with him driving the car from Canberra to Adelaide. Rollo and I would fly from Perth to meet him there, collect the car, and drive it across the vast Nullarbor Plain on his behalf, for his busy schedule prevented him from undertaking the long journey himself. It would take the entire four-day

Easter weekend, he estimated, for in those days, close to sixty years ago, the main section of the road between Ceduna and Norseman – out in the middle of the plain between the settled areas of South Australia and the outlying goldfields of Western Australia – was unsealed. One would have to drive with great care, especially where the rough road had been churned up by heavy haulage vehicles and reduced to troughs and ruts.

Paul explained all of this to us when we met him at Adelaide airport and made our way to the parking area where the trusty Peugeot awaited us. He handed Rollo a typed itinerary and laid out maps on the bonnet of the car with markings to show suggested sites for camping by the road. It would be up to us as to where exactly we stopped, and a matter possibly affected by contingencies along the way, from punctures to engine trouble, but if all went according to plan we should reach 2 Adams Road by late Monday afternoon, so Rollo wouldn't miss work the next day. The car would need servicing in the course of the journey, he said. Upon turning to his map, he pointed out the two or three places on the route where that could be done.

Rollo, the leader of our two-man driving team, nodded solemnly as all of this was unfolded. He was at the steering wheel as we waved goodbye and set off on our mission in a purposeful way, heading for Port Augusta at the head of Spencer Gulf. I was excited by the prospect of what lay before us, and slightly apprehensive. We had grown up in the era of the round-Australia Redex trials. Images of dusty vehicles careering along rutted tracks and through desolate hinterlands were still fresh to mind. But not to worry. The planning of our venture, it seemed, had been meticulous. We had our maps, our sleeping bags, cans of beans and other supplies in the boot, and some gas canisters for our tiny stove. All was in order.

We shared the driving but, even so, we drove a lot further than I had expected on our first evening on the road. We made an early start the next day and, with Rollo at the wheel, drove straight through Ceduna without stopping, although I would have liked to stop off briefly to look around the town. No way. Rollo was driving hard and fast. Our map and typed itinerary were there in the glovebox, but they seemed to have been forgotten. It gradually dawned on me that Rollo had a game plan of his own in mind.

At first, I thought his plan of action might in some way be inspired by the spirit of the Redex era, the need for any driver worth his salt to push ahead, hour after hour, fearlessly, disregarding whatever perils might lie in his path. This seemed to be so when we reached the unsealed section of the highway. The road running due west was roughly the width of an outback airstrip scratched out of the scrub but, in this case, with a churned-up surface looking like the remnants of a battlefield at Flanders. The way ahead consisted of a series of hard, rutted troughs and ridges, more or less parallel, but sometimes deviating sharply within the boundaries of the strip where a heavy haulage vehicle must have swerved sharply to avoid a pothole or a muddy patch. From time to time, no matter how vigilant the driver, our vehicle hit a pothole with a crunching sound or a savage thump.

We talked as we battled our way through this obstacle course which led inevitably to friendly chit-chat about Rollo's current girlfriend, the beautiful Delri Sullivan, who lived in North Perth. The more we talked – intermittently, of course, as the car was manoeuvred this way or that to avoid potholes or the occasional oncoming truck – the clearer Rollo's game plan became. He wanted to get back to Perth to see Delri as soon as possible. Some sort of get-together at her place in North Perth had been arranged for Sunday morning and he wanted to get back for that, before the Easter weekend ran out.

I reminded him that we were meant to be getting the car serviced along the way. Rollo nodded solemnly and agreed that it was the sort of thing that should be done. But when I asked him what exactly we were going to do about it, my question was left hanging in the air and the map with its various crosses and pencil marks stayed in the glovebox. We kept driving steadily onwards.

I can't say where exactly we finished up sleeping at night. The blinding sun due west, directly in front of us, slowly passed below the horizon, but we didn't stop till well after dark, flopping down in our sleeping bags beside the car. We spent one night on the outskirts of a mining township. It was a derelict scene with a headframe in silhouette against the moon and some youngsters dragging sticks along the corrugated walls of the shacks nearby. We bought a jerrycan of petrol and left at first light. We left the beans where they were and ate mostly at roadhouses.

When we reached Delri's place mid-morning on the Sunday, Rollo jumped out of the car, bright-eyed and bushy-tailed, as if our trip across the Nullarbor was a cake walk. I hung around as they chatted gaily. Rollo then felt obliged to inform me that he would be staying on for lunch and would need the car for a while longer. So I completed my epic journey across the southern half of the continent by catching a taxi home, leaving my co-driver at what was obviously, to his mind, the finishing line. Our trusty Peugeot, after all the ruts and potholes it had been subjected to, was never the same again, and had to be disposed of soon afterwards.

It was hard to say what my father made of our trip when he finally got back to Perth and managed to piece together the various fragments of our tale. Because he was on the conservative side of politics, journalists were always inclined to portray him as a stiff and probably judgemental figure (although he had been a journalist himself), but he wasn't like that. He was a poet at heart, and in his private life a free spirit with a sense of humour. Besides, he had grown up in an orphanage run by his Salvation Army parents. He had left them for greener fields but something of their credo remained. To judge people harshly wasn't much use. People had their faults. It was disappointing to say so perhaps, but naive to assume they would always live up to the standards expected of them. People were what they were. Which was why they often needed a helping hand.

So our weird trip across the Nullarbor, an adventure that has always stayed with me, did not, in the end, lead to recriminations on the home front, although, a few years later, when my father was minded to bring his Canberra-based station wagon across to Perth for electioneering, he put it on the train. In the meantime, unfortunately, Rollo's romance with the alluring, dark-eyed Delri had run its course.

By then, Rollo's interest in boating had persuaded him to buy a launch, small, but large enough to house a couple of bunks for sleeping and a tiny kitchenette to cover the needs of those aboard when the boat was taken on fishing trips to Rottnest or on the Swan River. It was named *Aristotle II*, not out of deference to the famous Greek philosopher but, rather, with a nod to Australian rhyming slang – Aristotle means a bottle. My diary for early January 1961 contains a few glimpses of Rollo's seafaring and social round at that time and the entries point to the temperamental nature of his boat and the suitability of its name.

14 Jan. Rollo, just back from Rotto, gave us a passionate but dire summary of the troubles he was having with his boat.

19 Jan. An afternoon card game with Rollo, Devo, Doc Davies, Stu Lang and Nons Nelson. Rollo went down heavily and as usual borrowed from me. I don't think he'll repay me, but it doesn't matter.

20 Jan. Took Rollo and the boys to the Rotto ferry at Fremantle.

22 Jan. Late afternoon went down and collected Rollo, Stu and Nons off the Islander ferry, plus some girl. We took the girl to Canning and went in for tea.

30 Jan. Down to Freo again to pick up Rollo, this time from the Temeraire ferry.

1 Feb. Went to Rotto with Slim Bower on the Triton ferry. Knocked down a few beers on the way across. Got settled on Rollo's Aristotle which was in a bit of a mess. We all went down to the basin and surveyed the talent. Discovered Jan Oldham was on the island. To the pub with Rollo in the evening. About 11.30 back to our bunks on board the boat, each bunk only a few feet above the bilge.

2 Feb. Went to the movies at the Rotto Picture Theatre. The usual rows of deck-chairs in the old iron hall, and quokkas in the aisle. Danny Kaye in Five Pennies.

3 Feb. A slack day. Mostly at the tearooms rolling cigarettes while

making facetious comments about the passing throng. Met Temeraire when it arrived at wharf. Stu and Nons had comes across to take the boat back, plus Neil Robbo. Went up the pub but a cop was there with an eye out for under-age drinkers no doubt, so we decided a tactful retreat was best. Found someone to get us a few bottles and went on to Bungalow 4 for a bit of a show. It was a rather macabre scene like something out of Erskine Caldwell's Tobacco Road – we sat round the table drinking beer and dipping into a brown paper bag full of pumpkin seeds. Our host was sickened eventually by his own supper, so we went back to the boat, not feeling too well ourselves.

4 Feb. We woke early, feeling bad – the dreaded pumpkin seeds. But we had to get going as Rollo and Stu had arranged for us to be towed back to the mainland by the Temeraire. We fastened on behind her as a crowd on the jetty applauded and nearby boat owners cursed. Set off. Quite a bumpy ride. The ferry left us beneath Fremantle bridge where Rollo took charge again. We were towed back to Claremont eventually by Bob Nunn. Anchor down safely at the mooring. An early night.

6 Feb. Went to the movies, then helped Rollo with an experimental bilge pump.

10 Feb. Went to cricket with Bob Keall to see our mate Sticks Brayshaw make his debut in the WA side.

11 Feb. The playroom at 2 Adams Road is a scene of desolation. The aftermath of Rollo's party, with beer bottles everywhere. Rollo flat on the bed at his end of the room, snoring heavily.

The scene I have just described reminds me of a similar set of circumstances that became an oft-told tale within our family circle. Parties in the spacious playroom at the back of the house were common at this time. On one occasion, as the four of us in the family – Paul, Alix, Rollo and me – sat down to a Sunday lunch in the dining room, being the day after one of Rollo's parties, my mother handed out dishes to the others at the table with a serve of what she described as a tasty veal dish, plus vegetables. She herself was on a diet at that time and was therefore confining herself to a glass full of a dietary beverage called Metracal. She gazed at us fondly, perhaps even enviously, as we tucked into our veal dish while she took a few sips from her glass.

Within a very short time, the three men at the table were exchanging apprehensive glances. The meal was ghastly, it was truly horrible, the taste indescribable. But we knew we couldn't offend the cook who had laboured to produce the tasty dish, so we did our best to persevere for a bit. Eventually, even Alix, still smiling benignly, felt obliged to inquire whether something was wrong.

'What did you say this dish was called?' Rollo asked cautiously.

'Veal marsala,' Alix replied.

Rollo glanced at his companions with even greater apprehension. 'Where did you get the marsala?' he inquired.

'There was a bottle of it in the playroom.'

At this, Rollo, almost at the point of spewing, dashed from the table, enough to persuade the remaining veal consumers to push aside their plates.

It turned out that in the course of clearing up after last night's party, throwing out the empties and so on, my enterprising brother had emptied the dregs and the slops from the miscellaneous bottles on the premises, and whatever remained in the coffee cups and olive dishes, into an empty bottle of marsala that had been left on one of the tables. He had never got around to throwing out that bottle too. It was left on a shelf with a cork in it. This was the bottle, labelled 'Marsala', that my mother had used to complete the preparation of her tasty dish. In Hasluck family folklore, this was always spoken of in hushed tones as 'the day of the Marsala'. Thanks for that, bro.

It has to be said also, as I ponder this incident, that Alix received some compensation in due course. She was working on a book at this time called *Thomas Peel of Swan River*, concerning a scheme devised by one of the early colonists to bring out hundreds of migrants to the Swan River settlement. The entrepreneur behind the scheme, Thomas Peel, encountered many difficulties including a shipwreck off the coast in May

1830. Alix's book contained a prefatory note with various acknowledgements.

> Last but not least I wish to thank my son Rollo for taking me cruising in his launch round Cockburn Sound in the track of the Rockingham, to reconstruct the conditions of its shipwreck, and for checking landmarks, currents and winds for me.

As the year ran on, Rollo broadened his range of activities and, outside office hours, began taking an interest in the theatrical world in Perth, which was quite lively at this time. His Majesty's Theatre at the far end of Hay Street, and the Playhouse Theatre in Pier Street, were the principal venues for productions. It was at the Playhouse in the early sixties that we saw various contemporary works from overseas such as John Osborne's *Look Back in Anger* and Shelagh Delaney's *A Taste of Honey*.

In addition, however, Frank Baden-Powell, portly with a huge moustache, was a force to be reckoned with. He had formed a group called Theatre 61, which put on plays in the Assembly Hall in Pier Street and at other places. Rollo auditioned and was selected for parts in Baden-Powell's productions of *The Hostage* and *The Quare Fellow* by the bad-boy Irish playwright Brendan Behan. These were followed by a small role given to him in Tennessee Williams's *Suddenly Last Summer* which was put on in the back garden of one of the old colonial mansions in Adelaide Terrace, a small dank arena with cast-iron balconies overhung with morbid foliage, reminiscent of the playwright's home town, New Orleans.

The cast of these productions, after the show, often finished up at the El Calib Coffee House in Hay Street, but now and again, at Rollo's suggestion, they finished up in the playroom at 2 Adams Road: Baden-Powell and his actress partner Eileen Collocott, Alan Cassells, Sally Sander, Morrie Ogden, Judy Nunn and a host of others.

Some years later, Judy Nunn went on to become a well-known actress on nationwide TV and then a bestselling novelist. The ever-resourceful Frank Baden-Powell expanded his vision by setting up the Hole-in-the-Wall Theatre (situated initially opposite Weld Square in Northbridge, then in Southport Street, West Leederville) and the more profitable Dirty Dick's Theatre restaurant chain, smoke-filled dives where bearded rascals in leather jerkins and buxom wenches in mob caps served pints of ale and so forth to supposedly Jacobean merrymakers, while performing some atrocious script riddled with double entendres and saucy backchat.

Rollo played a part also in a production of Arthur Miller's famous play *The Crucible* put on by the Patch Theatre Company in William Street. This was directed by David Crann, who ran Patch almost single-handedly for many years. At about this time, he invited his colleague, the artist Elizabeth Blair-Barber, to establish a small art gallery within the theatre building which added kudos to the Patch enterprise.

Many years later, when I was closely involved in the arts scene as a member of the Australia Council, I got to know David and had some interesting conversations with him. He was always intrigued by Rollo, he told me. Rollo always seemed to turn up to rehearsals in a fast car (but usually late) with an attractive blonde beside him, and full of tales about some recent adventure on Rottnest or in the city. He mastered his lines for *The Crucible* but only just in time.

The blonde mentioned by David was probably Rollo's latest girlfriend, Angela Watts, who lived quite close to us in Watkins Road, Dalkeith. For a time, they went everywhere together. The notion of an ever-present air of adventure may have had something to do with the sense of vitality affecting Perth as a whole, and the flow of unusual events.

The Russian sputnik satellite had circled the globe in 1957 and in April 1961 the Soviet cosmonaut Yuri Gagarin had become the first man in space. Then, in early 1962, the American John Glenn was rocketed into space from Cape Canaveral. Less than an hour later, his spacecraft streaked across the coast of Western Australia at Rockingham on the first of three scheduled orbits. A large number of Perth's 380,000 residents, in response to a well-orchestrated campaign in the media, found ways to turn on their lights for Glenn, some with lines of light bulbs draped over backyard rotary hoists. The BP refinery made a special effort to turn up its gas flare for the occasion.

As Glenn passed over the WA coast at more than 17,000 miles per hour, he told his fellow astronaut Gordon Cooper at the Muchea tracking station that he could see the lights of Perth. 'Thank you, everyone,' he said.

Perth became briefly famous as the so-called City of Light, a surge of fame that led to the Perth lord mayor, Sir Harry Howard, an elderly and somewhat dour municipal leader, being included in the ticker-tape parade through the streets of New York to honour John Glenn's achievement. The fuss made about all of this in the lord mayor's home town led to some ribald commentary and a round of memorable cartoons. I recall Rollo coming to our table in the kitchen one evening, grinning broadly, as he spread out the back page of the *Daily News* to display a sketch by Perth's leading cartoonist at that time, Paul Rigby. It showed two figures with uplifted arms on the back of a limousine being showered with ticker-tape and confetti on Fifth Avenue. The caption beneath the sketch had one New Yorker saying to another, 'That's Harry Howard from Perth, but who's the guy with him?'

The City of Light idea became part of the marketing strategies to promote the British Empire and Commonwealth Games held later in 1962 at the newly created Perry Lakes Stadium below Reabold Hill where we used to go horse-riding with the Acme Riding School. Another venue created for the games was the Beatty Park Aquatic Centre. From the stands overlooking the new pool, Rollo and I were lucky enough to see Dawn Fraser in action, including the moment when the famous Olympian came from behind on the final leg of the women's 4x100 yards freestyle relay to secure victory for the Australian team. The way she powered past her opponents was truly awesome.

It was in the lead-up to the games that a TV set entered our household. Most of our friends had sets at home by this time but we hadn't got round to it. But when my great-aunt Clarice Darker arrived from Brisbane to stay with us to attend the games – she was a sporting enthusiast from way back – the time had come to acquire a set so she could watch events for which she hadn't been able to obtain tickets or felt too tired to attend. We soon became accustomed to the 'box' in a corner of the living room and thus it became a permanent fixture.

It was probably just as well that the sweet-spirited elderly lady went back to Queensland when she did, for Rollo and his close friend Stuart Lang had settled down to building a new launch on the front veranda of 2 Adams Road. Yes, this veranda, with its fine view over Freshwater Bay, previously used by Paul and Alix to entertain their friends, especially on summer evenings, had now been commandeered by their eldest son for the construction of *Aristotle III*, a project that was meant to last only a couple of months but, as one month followed another, became eventually what seemed to be a dry dock voyage to uncharted realms, a never-ending saga. To me, a law student, it illustrated also the law of adverse possession: a veranda left unoccupied too long will eventually be taken over.

The construction of Rollo's new boat, and progress towards that end, was a constant talking point within the family. In the meantime, however, his trips to Rottnest in the existing vessel continued unabated. The 'bottle' concealed in the rhyming slang that had given the boat its name probably left a psychological imprint on the minds of Rollo's crew and others like them. A popular song for long-standing Rotto visitants – sung to the old Irish tune 'Galway Bay' – went like this:

> Have you ever been across the sea to Rottnest
> about the closing of the day
> to have a drop of cold Swan Lager
> and watch the sun go down on Thomson Bay.
>
> The Administration tries to make us see it their way.
> they hate us for being what we are.
> but they might as well go chasing after quokkas
> than try to keep us from our island bar.

The Rottnest Hotel – known as 'the Quokka Arms' – wasn't the only scene of action. By this time, Rollo had changed jobs more than once. He was now working for Custom Credit in Harvest Terrace, West Perth, just down the road from the state Parliament House. His employer, as its name suggested, was involved in hire purchase and other financing transactions. On his first day at the new office, Rollo got caught up in a conversational exchange in the men's toilet with a fellow employee freshly arrived from the United States.

When asked what position he held, Rollo said, 'Well, I guess I'm a kind of clerk.'

The American clutched his brow in apparent agony. 'No, no, no, no,' he shrieked. 'Get a grip, man. You're a junior executive.'

So that's what Rollo called himself thereafter. He was beginning to learn important things about the business world, he said, and the art of getting on.

Things were changing on the home front too. The so-called playroom out the back had been reconfigured so that the adjoining room where Rollo and I used to sleep in two single beds had become solely my bedroom and study, and a new space behind a partition at the far end of the playroom had been created for Rollo's bed and related wardrobes (one of which was filled with his spearfishing gear and the long metal canister and various gadgets comprising his underwater aqualung).

The reconfiguration didn't reduce the use of the playroom as a place of revelry. From somewhere or other, possibly from his American workmate – who was accustomed to describing himself, inevitably, as a senior executive – Rollo had picked up a book on mixing cocktails in the Manhattan style. This led to a small cocktail bar being set up in a corner of the playroom bearing a sign set at a rakish angle in gaudy Gothic script, 'Chez Rollo'. From time to time I was delegated to collect Rollo from his office at Custom Credit after work on a Friday. Our quick trip home was followed by a brief interlude in which Rollo laid out the makings before the arrival of some friends and workmates. Whisky. Gin. Rum. Brandy. Tonic water. Tomato juice. Slices of lemon and a bowl of ice blocks. The cocktail book open in front of him, he was soon dispensing various concoctions to an array of customers: Bloody Marys, martinis, screwdrivers, grasshoppers, Harvey Wallbangers, Tom Collins and so on. All the usual suspects.

There he was, not just a junior executive but, more importantly on a Friday night, mine host at Chez Rollo, surrounded by a convivial crew – David Knapp, Baden Bant, Ross Harrison, Stu Lang, Neil Robertson and various others – most of whom weren't backwards in comparing what they had in their glasses with what was in the book. Later, after they had all left, when Rollo and I sat down for a meal with Alix at the kitchen table, we were often well-lubricated, if not half-sozzled. But as Alix was a writer who often worked with a bottle of sherry on her desk, as an aid to inspiration, she didn't always pay close attention to the condition of those around her. She simply enjoyed the mood of jollity.

It may have been an evening like this that prompted Rollo to make an extraordinary purchase. He went over to a small car yard on Stirling Highway, opposite the commemorative Rose Gardens in Nedlands, to pay an instalment on a car he had bought. At the front door of the office, he found a bloke trying to sell the proprietor of the yard a clapped out old Chevrolet. There it was. A 1930s model. It had rusted running boards, battered paintwork, the doors creaked as they were opened, the stuffing in the leather seats was falling out, and there were cobwebs in various corners of the car.

The used car dealer said thanks, but no thanks. He wouldn't give two bob for it. The more they talked, the more it became apparent that the car owner had worked his way down from the northern suburbs, from one car yard to another, and had got much the same response wherever he went. He was about to give up.

Half-joking, Rollo said, 'I'll give you a tenner for it.'

The offer was accepted with alacrity. So, after making a phone call to a friend to drive the car he had arrived in, Rollo trundled back to 2 Adams Road in his clapped-out Chev.

Rollo had no real use for the Chev, and it quickly became apparent (not surprisingly) that it leaked oil and water. If, for example, one filled the radiator with water, it would be bone dry after a fifteen-minute run, which explained the half-empty jerrycans of water we found in the boot. However, as it happened, my daily trip to the Law School on the UWA campus took about fifteen minutes, so it would take only an initial filling up and one jerrycan of water to get me there and back. As an act of gracious magnanimity, Rollo agreed that I could have the use of his second car for the time being. We entered into a solemn pact that we would never spend a single, solitary penny on this strange, clanking ten-pound chariot with its incontinent radiator, and we never did. Parked on my parents' front lawn, not far from Rollo's uncompleted launch, the Chev was thought by some (Paul and Alix) to be an eyesore, but for a year or so, it proved to very useful, before its final demise.

Rollo's Chev gift was all very well but, to my mind, he still owed me. The day of the Marsala had not been forgotten, by me at least. Then, in my final year at Law School, he was given a chance to prove himself. I had been elected president of the Blackstone Society. The duties of the office included dipping into the society's budget to cover an ample supply of beer to Law School parties. Rollo was of considerable use in that regard as a person over the age of twenty-one years with access to a vehicle capable of carting kegs of beer from one place to another. This was the Land Rover my father had acquired to move around the bush tracks on his block of land at Kalamunda.

In those days, the standard fine for under-age drinkers was eight pounds eight shillings. Upon conviction, an offender became a member of the so-called Eighty Eight Club, which some youthful drinkers saw as a prestigious achievement. For myself, with a career in the law ahead of me, I had no desire to join the club. Rollo's help in moving kegs about the place was therefore much appreciated.

The Perth Ice Works in Murray Street, the Hotel Continental in Claremont, the Captain Stirling Hotel on the highway, Steve's on the foreshore at Nedlands…on various occasions throughout my final year the presidential Land Rover, often with Rollo at the wheel, would angle into the pick-up point at one or other of these establishments as kegs were loaded and the vehicle sped onwards to the site of a Blackstone Society shindig. But his principal moment of redemption was of an entirely different kind.

The main event on the Blackstone Society social calendar was the annual dinner which at that time was usually held in the South Perth Civic Centre. In the weeks preceding the crucial day, I became conscious of murmurings in the common room, a degree of discontent.

The annual dinner was a black-tie occasion and had followed the same format for years. Sherry. Dinner. Speeches. Tables cleared away. Dancing to the music of a local Glen Miller style jazz band – quickstep, foxtrot, charleston, some lively but essentially decorous rock and roll, a conga line now and again, and that was about it. But the times they were achanging. My political instinct told me as I monitored the common room murmurings that something new was needed, a radical masterstroke of some kind.

I consulted Rollo. He smiled, nodded sagely, and put me in touch with one of his former workmates: Johnny Young, a fresh-faced muso who had just assembled a fledgling rock group called Johnny and the Strangers.

The plan was quite simple. We would smuggle them in through a back door of the civic centre. The conventional band would play for an hour or so. We would then draw the curtains across the stage while Johnny and the boys set up their electric guitars and amplifiers. When they were ready, we would throw back the curtains, reveal the rock group, let them rip for half an hour or so to pacify the stirrers, and then go back to quickstep.

Need I say more. You can't go back. My committee, and even those who were pushing for something new with a bit of clout, had hopelessly underestimated the mood of change which the Beatles and others like them had set in motion.

The plan envisaged that when we threw back the curtains, I would make a brief announcement – 'This is a diversion, so what about giving these young musicians a break,' et cetera. Never was any speech so abruptly terminated. When the curtains were swept aside to reveal the big black amplifiers and the glittering drums and the zoot-suited, sequin-studded guitarists hunched over their instruments, the crowd went wild. Somewhere behind me a big, bold, booming electronic chord sounded, and my speech was history. As the throng careered on to the dance floor in a frenzy, for a mad, bad, exhilarating, microphone-in-hand moment, I felt like Lennon and McCartney combined. So I left the wild cavorting as it was. I let it be. The other band never made it back to the stage.

Thanks to Rollo, that was one of the highlights of my presidency and, in South Perth, probably the beginning of the sixties. Johnny Young certainly went on to higher things, including his long-running reign as a leading TV personality. In the days that followed, as I drove my old, battered, ten-pound Chevrolet to the Law School, taking care not to step on the rusted running board on the driver's side while alighting, I had to admit that Rollo had come up trumps. The day of the Marsala was forgiven.

But he may have doubted my forgiveness because it was at about this time that I pointed a loaded gun at him – the .22 rifle we had used for shooting rabbits and foxes in Canberra, a weapon that was brought back to Perth for recreational target practice on my father's Kalamunda block. It happened like this.

In late January of my final year at Law School, a number of people were shot dead at night in the western suburbs of Perth by a single unidentified gunman, some of them not far from where we lived in Claremont. They were random killings and there seemed to be a real likelihood that the serial killer would strike again. People were very nervous in the days and weeks that followed, and took various precautions.

At one stage, while my parents were away, Rollo and I began keeping our .22 rifle in the playroom, close to where we slept, in case it was needed, a box of ammunition nearby. On one occasion, shortly after midnight, I awoke to find a shadowy figure scrabbling at the window of my bedroom, a dark presence somewhere behind the Venetian blinds, muttering beneath its breath, while trying to clamber in. I leapt out of bed to get the gun and bullets. I shouted at the intruder to get back or I would shoot.

'Don't be bloody ridiculous,' the intruder said, before commanding me to open the window and let him in. It was Rollo.

I lowered the gun and did as he required. He had gone off to a party and forgotten his keys. A surrealistic moment, but nonetheless a close shave. It reveals also the mood of apprehension that had briefly gripped our neighbourhood. The nature of the times was graphically described some years later by the well-known writer Robert Drewe in his book *The Shark Net*. It emerges from his book that the killer was an inveterate night prowler called Eric Edgar Cooke, who was apprehended eventually and admitted to a number of murders and also claimed to be responsible for various hit-and-run attacks against young women using stolen cars.

As a former journalist on *The West Australian*, Rob Drewe was well-equipped to cover these events. He had grown up quite close to where Rollo and I lived at Adams Road and, like ourselves, was attuned to the delights of Freshwater Bay and was a fellow swimmer at Claremont baths. In his case, however, he was a friend of one of Cooke's victims and had a link to Cooke himself, who was an employee of his father's firm. In the end, after a jury trial and subsequent appeal, Eric Edgar Cooke was convicted, then executed, the last man to be hanged in Western Australia.

That wasn't the end of the matter. Cooke's confessions were thought to cast doubt upon the earlier convictions of a deaf and mute sexual offender Daryl Beamish for the murder of Jillian Brewer – found dead in her Cottesloe flat from wounds inflicted by a hatchet and a pair of scissors – and a young man, John Button, whose girlfriend was struck by a vehicle and fatally injured shortly after walking away from John Button's car in the course of a quarrel.

Many years later, when fresh evidence came to light, Beamish and Button were both acquitted by the Court of Appeal. The strange admixture of events comprising the Cooke, Beamish and Button cases were a constant talking point in Perth in the early sixties, and they were certainly of interest to all those who had been regular users of Claremont baths in their teens because, before his conviction, Daryl Beamish was often at the baths. When it comes to splashing about in a pool full of teenagers, one never knows, as to each of them, how things will turn out.

On the other hand, for Rollo to run the risk of being shot by friendly fire at 2 Adams Road while clambering through a window after midnight was not entirely surprising. The window belonged to what had once been his bedroom. Of greater relevance perhaps was the fact that he went out every night and was bound to forget his keys at some stage.

On some days after work, he would come home exhausted, or affected by a heavy cold or the onset of flu, and inform Alix and me that he intended to watch some TV after dinner and go to bed early. It never happened. After a bite to eat and a couple of phone calls, he would rally and set off to join some mates for a quick drop in the front bar of a local pub, or to check out a party. At the very least, on the basis that he would only be out for half an hour or so, he would leave to look at a few things on the boat, and be gone for several hours.

I always thought of this as just Rollo's way, his wish to pack as much as he could into every hour of the day. To a stranger, I realise now, it might seem that in Rollo's eyes there was nothing much for him at home; it was much the same as having a bed in the boarding house at school. He didn't really know what family life was like.

I will come to a moment later on when, unfortunately, Rollo's habit of going out again, trying to squeeze a little extra out of the day, feeling unwell or not, had dire consequences. For the time being, let me simply reiterate that, in all the years I lived with him at 2 Adams Road in the early sixties, he was never at home in the evenings, unless he was hosting a party in the playroom or a get-together around the bar at Chez Rollo.

Alix, now and again, would leave her typewriter to complain of his nocturnal habits. 'You're never at home!' she wailed. 'You're always out at night! We never get to see you!'

Rollo disposed of his mother's plea with his usual, good-humoured aplomb. 'There's a way of fixing the problem,' he said. 'If you want to see me at night, you can watch me sleeping.'

Moving On

I completed my law degree at the end of 1963 and a few weeks later, shortly before the Christmas break, I took the next step in my legal career by signing on to become an articled clerk to David Anderson in a local law firm, Lohrmann, Tindal and Guthrie. I reported for work early in the New Year at the firm's premises on the top floor of the Perpetual Trustees office block on the corner of Howard Street and St Georges Terrace.

Rollo and I were still living in the family home at 2 Adams Road. He was working in the city now for the market research firm AC Nielsen and was spending most of his time after business hours with mates from the boating scene, on Freshwater Bay and at Rottnest. We were both keen supporters of the Claremont football team, known as the Tigers, and as the football season got under way, we spent most of our Saturday afternoons showing our support.

I had applied for various scholarships to study overseas and was pleased to receive word early in the year that I had been awarded a travelling grant that would take me to Wadham College, Oxford, albeit with some extra financial support from Paul and Alix. I was booked to sail for England on the P&O ocean liner SS *Himalaya*, departing Fremantle 8 August 1964. I was pleased indeed when Rollo joined my parents in coming down to the port to see me off. He was full of plans at that time to set up a nightclub to be called Chequers as a way of supplementing his income or, putting it another way, as a means of financing the completion and running of the boat that had been slowly taking shape on the side veranda at 2 Adams Road, a launch to replace *Aristotle II*, destined to be called, inevitably, *Aristotle III*.

I found, upon leaving Fremantle, that there was a convivial bunch of fellow adventurers aboard the *Himalaya* – people of my own age off to London on working holidays or for further studies – including a couple of Rollo's friends, Jeff Lea and Bob Ilich. I kept in touch with Jeff and Bob after the ship docked at Tilbury and they became close friends of mine. In the course of my first year in England, they would often put me up at their flat in Parson's Green when I came down from Oxford to London, and it was much appreciated.

One of Rollo's oldest friends, Baden Bant, was in London on a working holiday. He was on hand to give me a quick introduction to London life when I first arrived. Within a day or so, he picked me up from the Norfolk Hotel near Australia House in the Strand and whisked me off for a night on the town. It appears from one of my letters home that we visited a place called the Rheingold Club (mostly frequented by German nationals), went on to the Zanzibar Club, and finished up at a place called the Black Sheep Club, which seemed to be filled with Australian dentists. Their services were in demand and they were all doing very well in London, making a hundred pounds a week, or so I was told. They had plenty to spend on entertainment.

We were drinking Swan Lager and Fosters, which was pleasing, but judging by the prices at the bar – as I discovered when it was my turn to buy a round – the Black Sheep Club was home to both sheep and wolves in sheep's clothing, the latter behind the bar, smiling wolfishly.

Baden drove me back to the hotel and dropped me off at about two a.m. It was locked up, with all lights out. I crept around the back and eventually found a door with a bell loud enough to arouse a nightwatchman. He quizzed me in whispery repetitive speech patterns as Peter Sellers or someone else from the *Goon Show* might have done while playing the part of an aged retainer.

A few days later – on a Saturday – I joined Baden and some of his dentist friends to watch a hard-fought rugby match between two local clubs. After the game, we went back to the clubhouse and swilled huge pints of English ale. It was like something out of an English movie, sitting there with a great pot of ale as those around me called out to passing players, 'Well done, lads,' or varying this with the occasional 'Never mind, Arthur' or 'Splendid show, Dennis.' It was beginning to strike me, accustomed by now to the black taxis, red double-decker buses, bowler hats and furled brollies, that the whole of England was like something out of a movie.

But the time for adventures and misadventures of this kind was coming to an end. My orientation week at the Norfolk Hotel, my initial base, was nearly up. So I found a cheaper room at East Croydon, just out of London, and a few weeks later moved on to Oxford.

In the meantime, much was happening on the home front of interest to me, and of importance to my enterprising brother. This emerged from the letters I received, the first of which arrived a month or so after I left Perth.

In a letter to me from 2 Adams Road dated 7 September 1964 Paul said,

> I came back to Perth on Friday night, but didn't see the football on Saturday as I had to do my duty at the opening of an aged persons' home in Subiaco. Claremont just scraped home from South Fremantle.

The letter turned to Rollo's ecstatic description of a goal by Kevin Clune.

> Clune got the ball with a nearly empty field in front of him, broke away, crossed the centre line, bounce after bounce, with the South Fremantle players chasing him and Claremont men shepherding off anyone who came within reach – bump, bump, bump, goes Rollo as the excitement of the story grips him, and then, having run over 100 yards, Clune kicks a beautiful goal before dropping down with the pack of pursuers on top of him. It saved the match. Claremont will play West Perth next Saturday.
>
> Rollo is in fine spirits. He is making money. The nightclub – I refuse, after having been in literary circles, to refer to it as Perth's latest nitespot – is doing well. Someone on the door was hit on the head with a bottle last week so it seems that people are really keen

to get in. Apparently the takings are quite good and the risk of losing (my anxiety rather than Rollo's) has given place to a certainty of making money. Perhaps some of the gains are illusory because, working hard at this, Rollo is not spending the fiver he usually spends each week and includes that among his takings.

His boat is coming along slowly but he was painting away at it all yesterday afternoon.

In a letter from Canberra dated 13 September, Paul added,

Before I left Perth on Wednesday evening I went down to look at Rollo's new boat – still in Des Piesse's workshop. It is coming along nicely and will be much roomier than the other, I think, although I took no particular measurements. It will be possible to close the door of the lavatory on oneself without taking off one's boots and curling up the toes.

In a letter dated 19 September, Alix observed,

Rollo's affairs are prospering. The nightclub is doing well enough to open only 3 nights a week now and still pay their way and profit. This gives the old boy a bit more sleep at nights. However, he's so pleased to have the money rolling in (and it does roll in because he keeps a large leather bank purse in our safe each night) and to have the cash to pay for the boat, which he is painting, but which will be in the water any day now, that he's positively angelic in disposition. At the moment, he's dating Gail Ruse.

But the dating scene was about to change. It was at about this time, with the football season coming to an end and his new boat nearing completion, that Rollo met Jill Munro. Brought up in the country town of York, to the east of Perth, Jill had been a boarder at Presbyterian Ladies College in Peppermint Grove, through to fifth form, and was now a trainee nurse at Perth hospital.

In later life, telling the story of her first meeting with Rollo, Jill recalled that some of her fellow nurses were in the habit of going out with a group of local lads. She thought of them as a bit too fast for her, but one evening she agreed to go with them to the Perth Yacht Club for some drinks. When she and the others arrived at the yacht club parking area, an Austin Mini pulled up nearby and the driver scrambled into view. She didn't know him but it turned out to be Rollo. He must have been working on his boat that afternoon because he was dressed in jeans and an old white windcheater marked by patches of red lead paint or some such and with tears in the sleeve. He was tall. He had a wonderful smile and great charm. As the evening ran on, she finished up having a meal with him instead of with his friend David Morrison with whom she was supposed be having dinner. He promised to keep in touch and did so.

In the meantime, the football season was brought to a triumphant conclusion. In a letter dated 13 October, Paul said,

> I flew back to Canberra yesterday after a hectic weekend in the West. Claremont won the premiership by four points, Brewer kicking the winning goal with only minutes – or it may have been seconds – to go. I couldn't see it for various reasons but Rollo was there. Two of your old school mates Brayshaw and Fairclough were in the team and did very well. The tiger presented to me by President Soekarno (stuffed) arrived in Perth on Saturday evening but I dared not give it to Claremont that night because it would have been hugged to death by the stampeding thousands at Claremont oval. I shall probably lend it to the Club at their annual meeting.
>
> On Sunday Mum and I flew down to Albany and back for the dedication of the memorial to the Desert Mounted Corps of the 1914-18 war. This is the piece of statuary that used to stand at Port Said but was wrecked by the Egyptian mob in 1956 during the Suez crisis. It was brought back to Australia in pieces and re-erected. Albany was chosen as the site because it is a memorial to the Australian and New Zealand soldiers and Albany was the place where the two convoys had their rendezvous before going overseas.

A little later, by a letter from Rome dated 24 October, written while travelling overseas as Foreign Minister, Paul added a footnote to the story of Claremont's magnificent victory:

> We left Perth last Monday afternoon. One of my last acts there was to present my Indonesian stuffed tiger to the Claremont Football

Club premises and by this time I imagine it has had more glasses lifted towards it than any other dead and stuffed animal in local history. We got into Cairo early on Tuesday morning.

These letters don't tell the full story. From what I heard later, I gather that Rollo's increasing interest in Jill Munro, the beautiful trainee nurse from Perth Hospital, had been moving on to a fully-fledged romance. They had been spending a good deal of time together and were beginning to look ahead.

Jill's father, Dr Jim Munro, had been a student at Scotch College in the 1930s and, after completing his studies at university and practising medicine in various places, he was now a general practitioner living with his family at 1 Elizabeth Street, York. Rollo and Jim shared an interest in fishing. Rollo got on well with Jill's mother, Lorna Munro, and Jill's three younger sisters, Jocelyn, Lesley and Dale. It wasn't long before Rollo and Jill were engaged.

I must now turn to the logbook of *Aristotle III* and some letters from home for a fuller picture of what was taking place. I will begin with Rollo's handwritten logbook, although it is important to understand that this purports to be simply a record of events at sea (admittedly of a somewhat unusual kind) and is therefore lacking in the finely wrought sentiment one is accustomed to find (according to the great works of literature) in the pages of a lover's diary. The personnel usually aboard the boat in 1964 were 'Skipper: RJ Hasluck. Crew: Stu Lang and Neil Robertson.' It emerges from the entries that the pub on Rottnest Island (the Quokka Arms), and the jetties where the ferries land, are situated at Thomson Bay, looking towards the distant mainland. Rollo generally set off for Rottnest from Claremont Yacht Club.

> 13 Nov. Departed CYC 7.30 a.m. Crew, Jill Munro, Fred Wells and Charles Clifford. Arrive Rottnest 9.30 a.m. After dropping Fred Wells went around to Longreach Bay where Charlie and Stu went ashore and won two hearts. From there proceeded to Little Armstrong Bay where 14 crayfish were speared. Returned to Thomson Bay. Had dinner and went ashore for a night of debauchery.

14 Nov. Arose late and after 'brunch' motored around to the Basin for a swim. As the swell was too great we again went into Longreach Bay where we played beach cricket and swam. Some fishing without much success was then done in Parakeet Bay. We returned to Thomson Bay for evening festivities.

15 Nov. Again arose late and went around to Longreach Bay where we tied alongside Dennis Inglis and had a pleasant afternoon in the sun. Charles Clifford went to church.

16 Nov. Arose late after a hectic party ashore on the Sunday night and immediately returned to the mainland, arriving at CYC 12.30 p.m.

22 Nov. Departed CYC, 10 a.m. with crew and Jill on board. Went to edge of Parmelia Bank in Cockburn Sound and fished for whiting. Total catch 2 dozen. Returned to Rocky Bay in the Swan River where catch was cleaned and we all had lunch. Returned to CYC 4 p.m.

6 Dec. Departed CYC 7.30 a.m. with crew, Jill Munro, Kaye Swinney, Gerry Bignall and Charles Clifford on board. To Carnac Island where we fished with no success, but due to weather conditions had to return to the shelter of the Swan River. We pulled alongside Dave Morrison on Faraway. Had lunch, swam, and drank booze. Returned to CYC at 4.40 p.m.

12 Dec. Departed 7.30 a.m. Arrived Rottnest 10 a.m. after fishing. A session at the pub with Alan Crewe, John Drinkwater, Jim Brandt and four friends. Around to the Basin after lunch where Stu tried unsuccessfully to pull some hearts. Returned to Thomson Bay for early tea then out to leeward side of Natural Jetty where we fished till dark. Caught one dozen nice Tailor.

13 Dec. At 3 a.m. Stu Lang came back to the boat where NAR and me were fast asleep. As the wind had swung to the S.E we decided to move the boat to a mooring. This was eventually executed after some rather hectic moments through all of which NAR slept soundly. Arose at 9 a.m. and went around to Little Armstrong where we speared a dozen crayfish. Returned to Thomson Bay for morning

drinks aboard Nimrod III before meeting the Islander at 11.30 a.m. with Jill aboard. Stu went off to get a girl called Val. We went swimming at the south end of Thomson Bay. At 3 p.m. we let Val off and set out for Fremantle. It was a rough trip and we were forced to stop on reaching the Harbour and pump out the bilge.

26 Dec. Boxing Day. Departed C.Y.C at 8.45 a.m. Crew only on board. Chris Johnson's dinghy and outboard motor in the cockpit. Perfect crossing on a flat ocean. Arrived Rottnest at 10 a.m. Went aboard Dennis Inglis' boat and had a few drinks with him. Then adjourned to the pub where we settled down to solid drinking. Around to the Basin after lunch where we swam for the rest of the afternoon. Tailor fishing about 6.30 p.m. About 8.30 p.m. went ashore to the pub. It closed at 10 p.m. and we all adjourned to Pine Cottage where there was a party. This we wrecked, along with most of the girls' egos. Hit the pit at 12.30 p.m.

27 Dec. Breakfast of Tailor fillets and toast. Met the Islander at 11.30 a.m. with Jill on board. Went up to Sandy Bay where we were joined by Mataitai and Nimrod III for lunch. A kip for a couple of hours then returned to the mooring where we went ashore and had a hot shower and a shave. At 6.30 p.m. we went out fishing for two hours and caught nine Tailor. Had fish again for tea and knocked off two bottles of 'Elephant's Donk'. Retired early.

28 Dec. Arose early at 5.30 a.m. to find our dinghy and outboard had sunk overnight. Retrieved both and spent two hours repairing outboard. Left Thomson Bay at 10.30 a.m. and went around to Parker Point where we swam and speared half a dozen crayfish. Returned to Thomson Bay at 1 p.m. for lunch and spent rest of afternoon in the pub. Dinner aboard the boat. It was a very quiet evening and we all turned in early,

A different and less graphic picture of the courtship emerges from the letters written to me by my parents. In a letter from my father dated 29 December – written a day after Rollo's 'log' peters out – Paul said this about his eldest son's activities:

Rollo's fiancée Jill had Christmas dinner with us. The Drake-Brockmans were with us too. Rollo has a look of manly solicitude and seems very happy. At first I thought it might be the new boat – which seems to be going well and to be a just cause of pride – but I really think it is the girl. Jill Munro is pleasant, good-looking, well-mannered and intelligent. I am a poor judge of these things but she seems to be well-suited to Rollo. Mum is delighted with her and is very happy indeed about the engagement. Rollo talks of a wedding about next April or May but, as he went off to Rottnest on Boxing Day, I haven't had a really good yarn with him yet.

In a letter written some weeks later, Alix said this:

On Xmas day after dinner we all, including the Drake-Brockmans, went down and climbed all over Rollo's launch. It is more commodious than the last one, but without the sink. The Monday after New Year Jill's parents came down from York for dinner here. It was nice but Jill who had just come back from Rottnest with Rollo wasn't feeling well. She asked for Dexal. At any rate it was nice to find that they are very agreeable people. Mrs Munro has had a rather strict Presbyterian upbringing and seems to expect more of Jill than I do. She thinks Jill and Rollo may be too alike. I wondered if she knew what I knew. When Rollo went off to Rottnest Jill was still on duty at Royal Perth Hospital. He lent her his car which she drove to Barrack Street jetty on the Sunday, parked it by a meter, and didn't return till Wednesday! In the meantime it had collected two parking fines. The inspector had found from the number that it was owned by Nielsen and had contacted Mr Milne, Rollo's boss, who rang me. I had to get Rollo called over the loudspeaker at Rottnest, but there was nothing he could do until the next day. It was a lesson to him not to lend the car, but Mr Milne was very decent about it.

In the same letter, after conveying some other news, Rollo's mother continued as follows:

Immediately after the hot weather Dad and I gave an engagement party for Rollo and Jill, for 60, held on the front lawn, starting at 3 p.m. We put on a buffet meal on the front veranda at 7 p.m. Afterwards six heavies lugged the piano out onto the veranda and, I am convinced, played it with their feet. The noise was terrific.

However, the Munros and Dad and I retired to the patio at the back and had leftovers and drinks in peace. They all went home at about 10.30, except a little knot of four who sat under Dad 's window till he got worked up because he couldn't sleep. He went out and asked them to go home. Rollo, who had departed to take Jill home, was mortified when he heard. However, it was a good party.

In a letter written at about the same time, Paul let me have his version of the party.

Fifty or sixty guests turned up. Eventually I sorted out a few whom I knew like John Nelson, Bob Keall, Geoff Eastaugh, Rod Newman, David Woodroffe, Neil Robertson et al but most of the others remained rather vague shapes at the far end of an upturned glass. I didn't lack for company, as every now and again, in response to urgent telephone calls, I went out to hold treaty negotiations with neighbours about parking on the street lawns. Rollo talks of a wedding in early April and is starting to look for blocks of land on which to build his house. What with, you ask? I think I must figure somewhere in the calculation.

My father may have spoken too soon. In a letter dated 24 January Alix said this:

Rollo has got a new job. I must say this for the old boy, he does get himself on with no help from Dad. This job is with a firm called Bowater-Scott, manufacturers of paper goods. They want a market research officer of their own. He was a bit young for the job, but had two interviews and then got it. They were pleased he was getting married – they like their men to be married because they're 'steadier'. Rollo said, joking: 'You mean I won't be coming to work with a hangover,' and the chap said: 'Oh, I do hope you drink. You'll have to entertain clients.' He need not have worried. Anyhow the pay is twenty eight pounds per week, and a Holden station wagon with all expenses paid. As you can imagine our boy is on top of the world.

Paul kept me abreast of the wedding plans in a letter towards the end of January.

Well, as you probably know, Rollo's wedding is fixed for April 14 in St Andrew's Church, Perth, with the reception to follow at that haunt of 21 year old celebrants – Chesterton Lodge. By a coincidence and not by any design the wedding takes place in the same church as the one in which Mum and I were married in 1932 and on the anniversary of our wedding. We got on a boat at Fremantle on the same day and went off for a year in Europe. Rollo and Jill are planning to leave the next day by air for Canberra. They can have the use of my little house there and that should give them a fairly cheap honeymoon as long as Rollo does not get too grand an idea and is just content to go picnicking and sightseeing day by day in the Peugeot. He is taking an option on a block of land at City Beach at a phenomenal price and I gather that this will be my wedding present to him. I will have a look at it when I get back to Perth.

Paul went on to say,

I had an interesting day yesterday down in Melbourne – Australia Day, January 26 – proposing the toast to 'Australia' at a lunch arranged by the Australia Day Association in the Exhibition Building. There were about 900 people at the lunch. The Association presented a medal to Dawn Fraser as 'Australian of the Year'. I had only seen her in the water before with her arms stroking and her heels fluttering and was very agreeably surprised and impressed. She made a very pleasant speech of thanks with a humorous remark here and there in an engaging manner. She looked well-groomed and quite self-possessed. I had wrongly imagined that in clothes she might look just like a big awkward girl and say 'Hi, Howjabie?' Not so. Never judge a swimmer by her splash. Then I had to hurry away and fly up to Canberra for a Cabinet meeting.

Paul's next letter, written a month later, was mainly concerned with the outcome of the WA election in which the David Brand Liberal government was returned with an increased majority. But he added this:

I didn't see much of Rollo during the weekend. On the Friday night though, he and Jill and their friends went to see 'Dr Strangelove' at the Windsor Picture Gardens. It happened that Mum and I went to see the same film and sat a few rows away, so I suppose you can say we had a family outing! We thought of you as we sat in the deck chairs in the warm and balmy summer night and wondered how chilled you were in your little room under the college roof. At home the patio is now occupied wholly by a nearly-finished up-turned boat – a dinghy about ten feet long that Rollo is building to service his launch.

He went on to say,

Today in Canberra Prince Philip opened the new Mint and afterwards we had him to lunch at Parliament House. It was a stinking hot day. Tony Manford, of Perth, won the Prince Philip cup for yachting with Leander this year and he came up to receive it from the Prince on Sunday. For the rest, life goes on. It is definite that I will be in London on 3 May. I hope you can come up to London to see me.

I turn now to a letter from my mother.

Well, Rollo's wedding day, at last, came and went! It was a very happy occasion. Henrietta Drake-Brockman, Nan Clifton and Mavis Chaney all helped me to do the flowers in the church. I was able to go home and have a rest before rising for the struggle of dressing. It was a full dress affair. Rollo and his friends hired tail suits. His coat was a bit big, I thought, and the collar didn't hide the tie round the shirt collar. However, there was nothing I could do about it, only trust most people would be too far away to notice.

Dad and I, true to form, arrived at the church too early, that is to say, ten minutes before the appointed hour of 6.30 p.m. And then we sat and sat, beginning to wonder if Rollo had got there, as he and the boys had left early to go to Chesterton Lodge and leave Rollo's car, and then with the others to drive him to the church. However, later it appeared that the delay was caused by Jill and a photographer who kept photographing her. She looked very lovely in pure white, and the bridesmaids in apricot colour.

All the usual gang of Rollo's friends were at Chesterton Lodge for the reception. There were about 90 altogether. The young couple got some marvellous presents, half of which are here and half at York. There were a few speeches and Rollo made a quite brief but neat one in reply. He and Jill went off at about 11.30 p.m. Next day they arrived back here and had a sleep preparatory to going off by air to Canberra where they are to have Dad's flat and car. He has also paid for them to have four days at the Hotel Belvedere in Sydney during that time. I am to give them a refrigerator when their house is built.

A letter from my father added some extra details.

I am writing this in the air between Perth and Adelaide. Having gone back to Perth for the wedding last Wednesday I hoped that I would be able to stay there for a while but various urgent matters have cropped up and I have to scoot back to Canberra for two days. I go back to Perth on Thursday morning to speak at the annual meeting of Curtin Division and then will fly back to Canberra on Friday. There is some heavy work waiting for me before I can leave for overseas on the 28th.

The wedding was a great success so everyone said. The bride looked lovely and the bridegroom was eminently respectable. The congregation in the church was dutifully attentive. Both sets of parents were very proud. Lots of photographs were taken on the steps of the church, no confetti was thrown, and then we went off to Chesterton Lodge to eat drink and be merry.

The speeches were few and brief. There was no telegram from you so I invented one, lodged it on your behalf and heard it read with all the pride of authorship. 'Good wishes et cetera, et cetera. Whose clothes has Rollo borrowed this time?' Stuart Lang was best man, Neil Robertson groomsman and Baden Bant and a couple of others were ushers. On Thursday night the carefree couple left for Canberra.

They returned from their honeymoon at the end of April. In the months that followed, they lived at 2 Adams Road, for Paul and Alix were mostly in Canberra or overseas at that time and the newly married couple were still making their way through various difficulties concerning the house they planned to build at 3 Dartmouth Avenue, City Beach.

Rollo settled down to his day job with Bowater-Scott, but was still restless. In June, he and his partners in Chequers nightclub decided to accept an offer for the sale of the business as a going concern. He was then minded to embark upon another venture: the establishment of a coffee shop at the Floreat Forum, a comparatively new suburban shopping centre in the vicinity of City Beach. It was to be called Chalet Coffee Lounge. An advertisement in the local paper, once the new business was under way, encouraged would-be customers to 'relax at the Chalet in the heart of the Forum for delicious coffee and tasty snacks'. It appears from the photo with this inducement that the coffee lounge had compact booths along both walls and a scattering of small, moveable tables in the centre.

In early October, Paul told me that

> Rollo has resigned from Bowaters in order to attend full time to his business interests. This has left him without the company's Holden to drive around in so he has taken possession of the family Land Rover, the vehicle from my bushland block at Kalamunda. Rollo is very happy and confident about his new venture and believes he will make more money out of it than he got at Bowaters. It's bit early to judge that. But he certainly likes being a businessman on his own. I do envy him his capacity to launch an idea with confidence. He has found another builder and another form of finance for his house at City Beach (after cutting out a few hundred pounds worth of space) and building should start this week.

Alix added some further details.

> Jill and I went to the coffee lounge to have afternoon tea one day. I must say it is very nicely furnished – green, thick carpet on the floor, plain white but nice thin china. Jarrah used with discrimination in the wall booths. Off-white walls with a few pictures, quite nice ones, which come from the Mona Lisa Gallery and are for sale. Rollo says he has sold one.
>
> With summer coming flies are a problem. He thinks he'll have to air-condition it, and he has had to put in a special low-temperature fridge for the cakes and sandwiches so they don't dry out. I am to give him a hundred pounds for that which I had meant to buy a fridge for their house with. He says he is making from fifty

to sixty pounds a day, but has a staff of 10, some of whom are on at night. He is keeping it open at night and on Sunday mornings. Jill and I were in it for about half an hour and there were about 20 people there. The whole shopping forum is a very nice one.

Things seemed to be moving on smoothly for the married couple.

In the meantime, as the year 1966 proceeded, I became increasingly focused on my own affairs. Mid-year, I passed my final exams at Wadham College, Oxford, and began looking for a job. I had met an attractive trainee teacher soon after my arrival in London, Sally Anne Bolton, whose family lived in the Cotswolds, near Stratford-upon-Avon. We were married by now and had decided to live and work in London for a while before I returned to my legal career with David Anderson at Lohrmann, Tindal and Guthrie in Perth. I was pleased to hear of Rollo's various successes and both Sally and I were looking forward to meeting Jill and other members of the Munro family. But not yet.

I found a job in Fleet Street and finished up working as an editorial assistant on *The Police Review*, the journal of the British bobby. From a flat in Highgate, our home base, Sally and I settled down to enjoying the London life.

Dartmouth Days

I came home to Perth in 1967 with my wife Sally Anne and our tiny, firstborn son, Anthony Guy Hasluck. My mother and Rollo were there to greet us at the crowded Fremantle passenger terminal. We found our way to the vehicles that would take us back to 2 Adams Road – Alix in the family sedan with Sally and Anthony; Rollo and I in the trusty Land Rover, on this occasion with an array of suitcases behind us, instead of kegs. We sat down to a convivial lunch in the dining room and a general swapping of news.

Rollo and Jill were now living in their new home at 3 Dartmouth Avenue, City Beach – a coastal suburb to the north of Freshwater Bay – with Melissa, their baby daughter. Jill wasn't available to meet us for a very good reason. Alix, in recent years, had been increasingly afflicted with hip trouble and found the social duties of a foreign minister's wife somewhat irksome. She had decided to solve the problem by grooming Jill as a suitable understudy. Jill was presently in Canberra with her father-in-law for social functions associated with a gathering of the Economic Commission for Asia and the Far East known as the ECAFE Conference.

Paul wasn't displeased with this arrangement. He had no objection to being seen at official functions with a good-looking young woman with a stylish taste in miniskirts. And, according to Alix, it helped to arrest the mad rush of media attention devoted to the women of Harold Holt's family in the year or so since Holt had succeeded Sir Robert Menzies as prime minister. Harold's elegant bikini-clad daughters-in-law were usually pictured knee-deep in the surf, the new prime minister in a wetsuit beside them, grinning broadly.

In the course of our homecoming lunch, as if to underline some of her jocular comments about the role of public relations in contemporary politics, Alix showed us a recent newspaper clipping.

A lovely young West Australian gave Indonesia's Foreign Minister Adam Malik a ministerial welcome today. Tall Jill Hasluck (22), model and daughter-in-law of the External Affairs Minister was second in the hand-shaking queue. Mr Hasluck took precedence but leggy Jill Hasluck got much of the attention. She wore a reddish costume, a definite four inches above the knee.

Jill Hasluck – the wife of Mr Hasluck's son Rollo – is in Canberra as a social replacement for Mrs Hasluck who is not well. Today, as Mr Malik's aircraft arrived, Jill was quite assured. 'I'm quite a veteran really,' she said. She had filled in for her mother-in-law once before during Princess Alexandra's last visit. 'I've got to learn all the names for these things,' she confided. 'Then it's just a matter of remembering their names and being charming – if possible.' 'She has no trouble about the charm', grinned the Minister.

Another clipping, not quite so brimful of charm, showed Paul on horseback in an old tweed coat and broad-brimmed hat, with some cattle mooching about in the background. The caption beneath the photo read as follows:

The Minister for External Affairs, Mr Hasluck, mounted on Ginger watches a cattle drive and muster at Booroomba near Tharwa. He and 400 other delegates to the ECAFE conference visited the 25,000 acre property yesterday for the muster, demonstration of sheep-shearing, spreading of superphosphate from the air and a barbecue.

Our lunch at 2 Adams Road was less than a barbecue, a light salad in fact, but an agreeable opportunity to find out what had been happening on the home front. It turned out that Rollo was presently working for an estate agency in Cambridge Street, Wembley, run by the family of one of my contemporaries from the UWA Law School, Tony Lennon.

Rollo had passed some exams, we were told, to become a commissioner for declarations, which permitted him to authenticate some of the supporting documents in property transactions. His main role was that of 'real estate salesman', a role with greater autonomy than that of a 'junior executive', he observed, but not entirely satisfactory. He was aiming to become a fully qualified real estate agent as soon as possible so he could set up his own firm and get going. Perth was expanding. Alan Bond and other developers were subdividing land all over the place. There was a smorgasbord of opportunities for anyone with an eye for a good deal.

Rollo explained all of this to Sally, the newcomer, as we drove across to City Beach. We surged up to the summit of Reabold Hill so he could point out various landmarks – the Perry Lakes stadium and Skyline drive-in cinema below the hill, the UWA campus by the Swan River at Matilda Bay, the faint outline of the city office blocks, and beyond them the long grey-green line of the Darling escarpment overlooking the coastal plain. Way off in the distance, to the north of the city, he added, lay the market gardens of Wanneroo, which were steadily being acquired and turned into new suburban areas.

Within a few minutes, we were surging up the driveway of Rollo's home in Dartmouth Avenue, a neat single-storeyed bungalow with a white exterior and terracotta tiles. It was new but under a cloudless blue sky typical of Perth, warmed by a bright afternoon sun, it had a Mediterranean look, a feeling underlined by the surrounding houses and a view of the sea, for this too was a recently created suburban quarter, and with the attraction of being close to the beach. In the living room, we were introduced to Lesley, one of Jill's younger sisters.

Rollo, still fully committed to showing Sally, his newly met sister-in-law from England, a sample of what Perth could offer, took us down to the beach for a swim. A drive-in cinema and a beach consisting of a long stretch of fine white sand, with a glimpse of Rottnest Island in the distance, were not new to me but certainly were to my English wife from the Cotswolds. But there was one thing I noticed that I hadn't seen before. As we left the parking area to reach the water's edge, I kept seeing here and there on the ground what appeared to be tiny silver rings, as though various women had absent-mindedly stripped rings from their fingers while walking along and left them where they fell.

I picked up one of the rings. Sensing my puzzlement, Rollo explained that these were simply the rip-top metal tags one used to open beer cans or cans of soft drink. This moment of enlightenment wasn't a matter of any importance, just a tiny sign of the way things can change almost imperceptibly if a traveller stays away from his home town for a number of years. When I left Perth, one drank from bottles. Now it was cans. So be it. And the surfboards around me had changed too. Lighter and sleeker. And it seemed that some of the surfies aboard them were local heroes, admired by all and sundry.

A change of far greater significance was the move to decimal currency that had taken place in my absence. Pounds and shillings had been replaced by dollars and cents. Sally and I had to get used to handling the new notes and coins, thinking in tens. Nonetheless, with a nod to tradition, she kept a few sixpenny pieces that were still lying about the place on shelves or at the back of drawers. These were buried in Christmas puddings over the years to keep younger members of the family circle happy.

I found that not much had changed at my law firm – Lohrmann, Tindal and Guthrie – when I went to the city on the day after our arrival. The firm was still housed on the top floor of the old, seemingly gothic Perpetual Trustees building on the corner of Howard Street and St Georges Terrace. It was close to a number of other law firms in that vicinity and near the group of lawyers, headed by leading advocates such as Francis 'Red' Burt and John Wickham, who were now practising solely as barristers. They spent their days in court. They would take instructions from solicitors only, not directly from clients. The senior partner in my firm, Hugh Guthrie, was still in the state parliament as the member for Subiaco. The firm was still being run essentially by David Anderson, the partner responsible for supervising my work as an articled clerk.

My two-year term as an articled clerk had been interrupted by my time overseas and, subject to the passing of some further exams, it would be another year or so before I could be admitted to the Bar as a fully qualified legal practitioner. On my walk to the Barristers' Board to check these details, I chanced upon various contemporaries from the UWA Law

School, a number of them now fully fledged practitioners, which was galling in some cases as they proceeded to dwell upon their successes in court. At a dinner party in the evening, I introduced Sally to some of my close friends from UWA days, including Geoff and Sandra Miller, and Fred and Angela Chaney. The Chaneys had just come back to Perth after a few years in Papua and New Guinea. Not surprisingly, Fred had many tales to tell about prosecuting cases in remote regions.

We were introduced to Jill a few days later when she got back from Canberra, full of tales about the ECAFE conference. She was warm and friendly and we got on well. When Paul returned, the family was joined for dinner by close friends of my parents, Geoffrey and Henrietta Drake-Brockman. I see from the diary I was keeping at this time that halfway through the dinner Rollo's friend Tony Unmack arrived to whisk him away to the Claremont Speedway, where an important race was on.

After dinner, the rest of us drifted out to the front veranda, once the scene of Rollo's boatbuilding operation, but now a pleasant vantage point from which to view the last of the sunset and the evening stillness of Freshwater Bay. It was fascinating, as we sat there, to hear Henrietta describe the research for her book *Voyage to Disaster*, which had led to the discovery of the *Batavia*, a Dutch shipwreck on the Abrolhos Islands to the north of Perth. After a while, we drove Jill back to Dartmouth Avenue, where we waited for Rollo to appear.

Sally gradually became acquainted with our habits and familiar haunts, including my father's block of land at Kalamunda. We drove to Mandurah for a barbecue with Rollo and Jill at the Munro holiday house, followed by drinks with his friends Dave Rosenbrock and Tim Knowles at the old Peninsula Hotel. We took the *Islander* ferry to Rottnest, where Rollo and Jill had rented a cottage on the road to the bakery and general store, an avenue overhung by the dark green foliage of massive Moreton Bay fig trees. With Melissa and our son Anthony looking on, we were fascinated to see Rollo go out on one of the reefs with a net and spear and within a very short time come back with a small octopus squirming in the net and a couple of crayfish. These we had for lunch.

In office hours, I was settling down to an array of files and related legal work at Lohrmann, Tindal and Guthrie. At the end of the day, I went off to lectures leading up to my end-of-year bar exams. From time to time, Rollo would appear at my desk in the Perpetual Trustees building for some legal advice. Now and again, on the social front, we joined Rollo and Jill for dinner at Dartmouth Avenue, or for an outing with the kids. By this time, Rollo's friend, Tony Unmack, an experienced car dealer, had helped us find a car we could afford, a dark blue 1950s Morris Minor with a rounded bonnet and a tiny boot. To signal a turn, it had wee small yellow indicators that flipped up from each side of the vehicle like semaphore flags waved by a leprechaun.

It wasn't long before Sally and I moved out of 2 Adams Road. With Rollo's assistance, as a knowledgeable party in the real estate game, we found a home for ourselves in rented premises at 3 Brown Street, Claremont, an address lying between Adams Road and Dartmouth Avenue. It was a small, older-style house with a hot-water system worked by a dilapidated chip-heater.

Rollo claimed to know all about chip-heaters. He assured us that virtually any kind of fuel could be used to keep the fire below this incredible contraption burning brightly, from a few sticks of kindling to scraps from the kitchen such as peanut shells or potato peel. Knowing Rollo, we weren't quite sure whether this was sincere hyperbole or simply one of his quasi-satirical impersonations of an agent damning a property with faint praise as a tactic to improve his negotiating position.

Rollo had been with us frequently in recent weeks as we inspected various properties and, at the end of the day, over a drink or two, we had seen his imitation of an agent's blatantly self-interested approach to negotiations, although we never found out whether he had ever employed these tactics in actuality. Many years later, in a novel I wrote about the outlandish WA Inc era in Perth, I reproduced the general flow of Rollo's satirical sketch.

> The agent parted the coat flaps of his suit, placed his hands on his hips, and looked around the room, non-committal, but eyebrows raised.

'Nice view', he said to the man behind the desk, while staring at the dingy light-well.

Then, without lowering his eyes, he tested the floor beneath his feet, jackbooting one foot up and down on the same spot, making the desk rattle.

His brow registered doubt. Suspicion. He looked down and, warily, leaned his weight forward on that foot, pressing down on the carpet just in front of him, rocking the weight of his body to and fro on the one spot, knee bent, probing the area of suspected weakness.

'You pay rent for this?' He looked up, but still maintaining the half-crouching position.

'Yes. As a matter of fact, I do.'

The agent quickly sucked in air through pursed lips. A wincing, whistling sound. 'Ouch!' he exclaimed. 'The day of the peppercorn!'

Slowly, he straightened up. He eased one of the chairs out from his side of the desk, inspected it for dust, dusted it, and sat down. 'I thought you said you were opening a new office?' His voice was tactful, but concerned.

'This is it.'

The agent whistled inwards again – louder, but lower, the pain stabbing deeper. His eyes wandered around the room sympathetically – ceiling, floor, the light well. He let his breath out softly through stupefied lips. 'So this is it.'

He slumped backwards in his chair, legs going limp, fingertips collecting beads of invisible sweat from his brow, disposing of them with a despairing gesture. 'So this,' he sighed, as if a noose were being fitted to his neck, 'is it.'

Upon reflection, as I revisit this highly embroidered scene, I doubt that even Rollo, notwithstanding his customary zest, his sheer effrontery on occasions, would have had the gall to carry on like this in actuality, although his sketch certainly seemed real when presented to family or friends over a drink. He had to make a living, after all, and an offcut from his theatrical days such as this would do little to advance his career in the hard-nosed business world.

But there was an echo of his act on the day he took me to a demolition contractor's yard to look for doorknobs and some other bits and pieces that might prove useful while we were fitting out our rented premises, getting the chip-heater into working order.

'You've got a good hand there,' Rollo remarked as the contractor spread out some old doors for our inspection like a poker player displaying a pair of aces or a flush.

Most of the doors were paint-blistered or buckled, but the contractor seemed pleased by what had just been said. 'Yeah!' he agreed. 'A good hand.'

It may have been this, Rollo's backchat, his ability to keep people entertained, or engaged at least, that led to him being recruited to act as a master of ceremonies at the Red Cross Ball held at York, a popular social event put on each year in the majestic town hall in Jill's home town. Sally and I were invited too, so arrangements were made for Melissa and Anthony to be looked after by babysitters while a group of us boarded a bus that Rollo and Jill had chartered for the journey to York.

The bus, with an amiable driver at the wheel, headed east to the Darling Range and passed through Kalamunda and Mundaring with an air of purpose, but as we approached the pub at Sawyer's Valley there was a feeling amongst certain members of the group that it was time for a stop. We had been travelling for an hour or so, perhaps even longer a voice from the back surmised, and we were seriously in need of hydration – dire need, the same voice insisted.

Inside the pub, with a row of middies lined up along the bar, various members of the group soon began to speak well of life in the bush, the great outdoors and all that sort of thing. Which led to another round of middies. As we boarded the bus again, I was beginning to wonder whether Rollo might be overly fortified for the role ahead of him. But in no time at all, or so it seemed, we were disembarking at Jill's home in York where we were greeted by her parents, Jim and Lorna Munro, and her attractive sisters. The mood of well-being was such that the voice from the Sawyer's Valley stop, proposed a couple of nerve-tighteners before we gathered for the pre-ball drinks. So the blokes in the group adjourned to the York Hotel for the next hour or so.

Arrangements had been made for some of the out-of-town visitors to be billeted at various locations. Sally and I were driven across town eventually to the home of Paul and Libby Monger. The Mongers had been early settlers of York and Paul and his brother Rodney, both about our own age, were farming the family property near Mt Bakewell. After a shower and a quick bite to eat, Paul and Libby drove us back to the Munro household, where a throng had assembled for pre-ball drinks. By the time we made our way to the town hall, we were all in a merry mood.

It emerged, after a few speeches, as the dance band began to make its presence felt and the ball got under way, that the proceedings were to include a beauty pageant of some kind in which a bevy of contestants would appear one by one and glide down the dance floor to the cheers and applause of the onlookers. The scene had been set by the arrival of a small carriage, or pony trap, conveying Rodney and Frishie Monger to the front door of the hall. Rollo, the previously appointed master of ceremonies, was now, after our various lubrications earlier in the day, well primed to perform his special role.

When the time came for the pageant, Rollo mounted the stage, dragged the microphone stand towards him, and made some welcoming remarks in the style of his favourite comedian at that time, the American stand-up comic, Shelley Berman, although Berman was mostly perched on a bar stool as he distributed his gags. Fortunately, the well lubricated throng in this venue, was prepared to laugh at whatever was said. Off to a good start, Rollo was soon proclaiming the merits of the various contestants, most of whom, being local girls, were well known to the enthusiastic onlookers.

'Here comes Jane X,' he would say, 'looking pretty as a picture.' Or 'A big hand, please, for Jenny Y.' To which he might add, Shelley Berman style, 'Which means clapping, nothing more.'

Repartee of this kind was still permissible and seen simply by most people as good, old-fashioned knockabout humour. On the whole, he handled the occasion with finesse, including the final presentation of an award. He had kept the crowd entertained and that was the main thing.

Next morning, the entire group, locals and visitors, set off for a picnic at some waterfalls on a farming property on the road to the neighbouring town of Northam. It was a beautiful day. Everyone milled about while a steel keg of beer was rolled into view and a fireplace for a barbecue was quickly assembled from stones lying about the place. Sticks were gathered for the fire.

This was an opportunity for Sally to learn more about Australian habits of speech and ways of doing things. To her surprise, there seemed to be very little water running over the so-called waterfall. She was equally surprised to see the keg, now speared and ready for use, positioned in a shallow pool beneath the flow for cooling purposes. It was of interest also to see a ploughshare, smeared with fat, flung on the rocks around the fire, soon to be sizzling with a wide array of chops and sausages. Bread rolls and salad bowls were produced, chairs and picnic tables unfolded. A few hours later, we restored the picnic area around the little waterfall to its original state and were on the way home to Perth by nightfall.

A barbecue of charred chops and sausages was not the only area of surprise in the field of culinary delights. Jill had begun doing some modelling at this stage of her married life to earn some money. A photo of her appeared in the local press which was destined to pass into family folklore. She was presented to the viewer wrapped in an aluminium foil miniskirt with one hand hovering gracefully above a dinner plate bearing a trussed-up cold chicken. The caption below the photo was brief but possibly enough to inspire a monologue in the Shelley Berman style.

> In these days of ad lib fashion, it's a toss up which chick gets to wear the aluminium foil first. In this case, it's lovely Jill Hasluck of City Beach. A few days ago there was a London picture of a model wearing an aluminium foil dress which it was said could also be used to cook the festive season chicken in: Jill had already beaten London to the punch. She wore a similar outfit in a city parade recently, then cooked dinner in it.

Political correctness hadn't been discovered back then, and people were still inclined to look for the humour in a situation and to laugh along with whatever was meant to be amusing, or treated as just good fun, from what was said at beauty pageants to unusual photos and write ups in the press. Then, unexpectedly, at the end of 1967, the political scene in Australia was suddenly darkened by a tragic event, a matter that had a particular significance for our family circle. The prime minister, Harold Holt, lost his life while swimming. This led immediately to speculation about who would take his place.

The unusual circumstances of Holt's death are well known. A keen swimmer, he entered rough surf at Cheviot Beach near Melbourne at about noon on Sunday 17 December, unaccompanied, and was never seen again. While the search was still going on, the Governor-General, Lord Casey, commissioned Deputy Prime Minister John McEwen to form a caretaker administration until the Liberal Party – the dominant party in the conservative coalition – could elect a new leader. My father was one of the senior ministers who decided to stand for the leadership, the other candidates being Senator John Gorton, Bill Snedden and Leslie Bury.

We hoped Paul would win but, as one day followed another over the Christmas period and early in the New Year, before a ballot could be held in the party room in Canberra on 8 January, the outcome seemed uncertain. We wished him well when he set off for Canberra shortly before the fateful day.

In the end, in the final ballot between the two candidates remaining in the field, Gorton and Hasluck, the former was elected leader by an estimated margin of five votes out of the eighty-one votes counted. *The Sydney Morning Herald* carried this report:

> On Tuesday the Liberal Party voted for adventure. It chose the daring man, Senator Gorton, as against the safe man, Mr Hasluck. Only time will tell whether this was wise, but there is no doubt that in electing Senator Gorton as their leader and Prime Minister the Liberals have set a fresh wind blowing through the corridors of power.

Of all the candidates Senator Gorton had the most personality, the greatest public appeal, the most political flair. He is perhaps the best debater on the government side in either house and the best equipped to take on Mr Whitlam. What is less certain is whether he also has the tact to handle a team of ministers and to repair the coalition with the Country Party which is more precarious than at any time in many years.

In a personal letter to the former prime minister, Sir Robert Menzies, my father provided a fuller picture of the contest and of factors underlying the final ballot in the party room.

> Now that the party meeting has become a piece of political history I thought I should like to write to you and thank you for the encouragement and support that you gave me. The talk we had together at your home on Tuesday of last week will always remain in my memory as a treasured and quiet pool of friendship.
>
> Shortly before the vote was taken I was much more hopeful than the result justified as I had continued to receive strong expressions of support from persons, both inside and outside the party, whose judgment I rate highly. I had the illusion that some of this regard for me by persons with experience might have communicated itself to the generality of members. That was not to be the case. Looking back, I can see now that when three streams join they are likely to make a much bigger flow than a single stream. I was depending on a single stream of support. Gorton managed to combine the anti-McEwen stream and the pro-McMahon stream and several minor creeks with his own body of support.
>
> The question that remains to be worked out is whether the new prime minister will be equally subtle and determined in disposing of McMahon. I doubt whether he can because he has come to office by working in collusion with McMahon to some extent. The extent of the collusion was more clearly apparent in the actions of Gorton's supporters than in Gorton himself.
>
> As you may have been aware, we were moving towards difficult times even before Harold's death. If Harold had lived I think we would have been in a dreadful mess within the next six months. One of the major contributions to that mess would have been the

persistent disloyalty of McMahon to Harold and McEwen as well as to senior colleagues. I do not think that the recent experience has in any way chastened McMahon or changed his nature.

I am sure you will realise from our old association that there is no bitterness or rancour in my summing up of the situation. At moments I feel that Alix and I have been lucky to escape a fate worse than death. I thought, however, that you would be interested in frank comments on the situation and the reason why I did not get the numbers. It was simply, as I see it, that I had only one single stream of support.

Later, in a mood of introspection, as reflected in his autobiography *Mucking About*, my father dwelt upon some other very personal but probably significant matters that may have had a bearing upon the contest and contributed to his feeling of comparative calm once it was over.

As a young man never did I hope or intend to have a career in politics. I never joined any political party. I became keenly interested, first as a reporter and then as a post-graduate student in what was going on in politics, but I took no part in it myself. My Salvation Army parents, like so many people who devoted themselves at that period with much self-sacrifice to helping the under-privileged, the outcast and the unfortunate, knew more of the frailties of the working class than of their capacity, although this was qualified by a faith in education: if a man improved himself by education than he might be worth electing. Many years later, when I had become an active parliamentarian, I realised one day that another earlier influence that left me unfit to be a politician in Australia was Montaigne. He entertains ideas about all sorts of subjects. His curiosity is universal. He muses on the vanity of human wishes and the transience of fame. Montaigne refreshed my mind and calmed my spirit.

It will be apparent from this brief excerpt drawn from a chapter containing longer reflections that, in addition to matters mentioned in the letter to Menzies, there were probably some deeper factors weighing against Paul Hasluck. Unlike many parliamentarians on the conservative side, he didn't have any direct experience of or close connections to the business world. He was an intellectual and, by reason of his upbringing, he was mainly concerned with social justice. All of this probably set him slightly apart from others in the party room.

Various political commentators have said that Hasluck should have tried harder to garner the votes that would have carried him across the line. He should have done more by way of scratching backs, making ingratiating phone calls, offering cabinet positions or overseas appointments, coming up with promises of one kind or another, even though many of them would have been difficult, if not impossible, to keep, for that is the nature of the political game.

I smiled wryly at all of this back then, and continue to do so. The media pack are constantly denouncing back-stabbing aspirants for high office in a pious tone, insisting that the Australian public deserves better: leaders with a track record of integrity and competence. But then, curiously, the same reporters become even more indignant if a candidate appears who doesn't get up to the usual tricks. What's wrong with him or her? You can't expect supposedly experienced parliamentarians to look at the field and just plain make up their minds! No way. The candidate should be out there at the track, charming the stewards and punters, networking and conniving, doing what has to be done. All too often, the media pack pontificates about the need for good government, a firm seat in the saddle, calm and efficient leadership et cetera, but finishes up backing the colt from charisma, the candidate with flair.

Rollo and I tossed around ruminations of this kind for a few days, intensely disappointed by the result of the party room ballot, but life goes on. It was comforting to learn, as put to us by Paul himself when he returned from Canberra, that our man had accepted the result calmly and had agreed to carry on as External Affairs Minister in the Gorton government. It is a well-known fact, of course, that as things turned out, Gorton couldn't control McMahon and some years later, having mustered sufficient support in the party room, McMahon got rid of Gorton. His guile paved the way to a Labor win under Whitlam and probably inspired the spate of leadership challenges that has plagued Australian politics ever since.

For Rollo, however, throughout 1968, politics wasn't his principal concern. The business world in Perth was on the move and he wanted to be part of the action, without delay. With these thoughts in mind, he went into partnership with a friend of his, Philip Trouchet, who was already qualified as a real estate agent, and within a short time Rollo was managing an estate agency called R.J. Hasluck and Associates. They had an office in Cambridge Street and began looking for business, not only sales of residential properties but also opportunities to acquire land fit for subdivisional development.

I had passed my final exams by now and was admitted to the Bar in the course of the year. I had been sidelined into what I saw as an unduly subordinate role at Lohrmann, Tindal and Guthrie, with the result that my situation in the firm wasn't entirely satisfactory. In an era when land transactions were still being handled exclusively by lawyers, rather than by settlement agents – a change to legal practice that came later – Rollo began turning some conveyancing work in my direction. From time to time, he suggested that I should 'go out on my own' or, at least, move to another firm where I would be free to service his needs without restriction.

I was feeling restive, but not quite sure what I should do. I ignored Rollo's suggestions for the time being and stayed where I was. Until, as the result of casual chat on a social occasion, I agreed to meet a friend for lunch and was presented with a proposition of an unusual kind, from a completely unexpected quarter.

Visions and Investments

The grey, unwashed, second-hand Mercedes pulled into the kerb outside the Perpetual Trustees building in St George's Terrace. The driver beckoned. I didn't recognise the man at the wheel at first. He was wearing dark glasses and one lens was cracked, giving the driver and odd, less than impeccable appearance. Besides, knowing that the man I was waiting for, until, a few months ago, had been, like myself, an articled law clerk, I was expecting a smaller car.

The driver beckoned again and smiled, so I clambered in. Yes, it was Rob Holmes à Court. The fact that he was half an hour late for our lunchtime rendezvous removed any lingering doubt as to his identity. A few years ago, we had been in the university debating team and I knew that time meant nothing to my companion. He was always late, and when he settled down to the matter in hand, he took as long as he wanted. Punctuality was just a convention and, as artists and adventurers know, the rules and customs of society shouldn't be taken too seriously. That was why Rob had agreed to meet me for lunch: to find out whether I thought as he did.

We had a counter lunch at the Floreat Hotel in Wembley and I listened while Rob talked. Within twenty years, my friend from Law School days was destined to become the richest man in Australia, but the proposition being put to me across a laminex tabletop in the lounge bar of the Floreat Hotel contained no hint of what was to come. He had just set up his own law firm and, today, the crucial question was whether I would be prepared to join him. If I brought in my brother Rollo as a client, with conveyancing work from his estate agency, that would be a plus. My former debating teammate spoke quietly, persuasively.

Rob had been brought up in Rhodesia (as it then was) but had gone on to attend the exclusive Michaelhouse school in Natal, across the border in South Africa. For some reason which was never quite clear to me, he had found his way to New Zealand and studied agriculture at Massey University. In 1962, by now four or five years older than the average first year student, he moved to Perth and began a law degree at the University of Western Australia. I was two years ahead of him at Law School, but younger. He was a skilled debater and soon became leader of the university team. Tall, debonair, given to underlining his points with graceful movements of the hand, he was eloquent and very effective.

It was hard to resist such a man. Although I hadn't seen much of Rob since our debating days, I was, towards the end of our lunchtime meeting, intrigued, then finally tempted by his proposition.

Looked at objectively, he didn't really have much to offer. After graduation he had spent a few months as an articled clerk with a well-known firm, Keall, Stable and Brinsden, but had fallen out with his principal. Rob's version of the disagreement was that he used to return his pay packets to the bookkeeper unopened, on the grounds that the pittance being offered was, quite simply, ludicrous. This extraordinary behaviour led to ill-feeling with the result that Rob transferred his articles to a sole practitioner's firm elsewhere in the building. By the time he finished his articles, he was running a branch office for his new principal on the understanding that he would take over that section of the practice the day after he was admitted to the Bar, and thus entitled to practise law on his own. The takeover, the first of many in years to come, had been accomplished a few months earlier and the proposal was that I should join the fledgling outfit, which would then be known as M.R.H Holmes à Court & Co.

Rob might not have much to offer but, shrewdly, he had approached me at just the right moment. I had two law degrees but the firm I was with seemed to attach little importance to them, and the work assigned to me wasn't to my liking. I was in a mood to strike out on my own, aware that Rollo would be a source of at least some incoming instructions.

It might be easier to make a fresh start if I joined a friend from other days with similar aspirations and a firm that was already up and running. Besides, the story about the unopened pay packets being returned had awakened the contrarian within me. So I said yes to Rob. He could count me in.

It turned out that M.R.H. Holmes à Court & Co. occupied three rooms and part of the ladies' powder room on the second floor of what was then Pamos House at 249 Adelaide Terrace, on the outskirts of the central business district. Rob's office was flanked by a smaller room which housed his loyal secretary, Val Pitman. My room was a few paces away on the opposite side of the corridor. Rob's wife, Janet, acted as an extremely efficient office manager, and we had an outside girl to attend to settlements and do the filing. Our bookkeeper, who came in two days a week, worked in an antechamber attached to the ladies' powder room. As time went by, this bizarre location began to get her down so she moved into a corner of my room.

Realising that the work available to a fledgling law firm might not be sufficient, Rob had opened a so-called branch office at Esperance, six hundred kilometres away on the south coast. The idea now was that the two practitioners in the firm, Rob and myself, would take it in turns to man the branch office for a few days every month when the magistrate came down from Kalgoorlie to attend to the court list.

But Rob soon tired of the cramped office space at Pamos House. He told me one day that he had signed a contract to buy a property further down the road at 168 Adelaide Terrace, a small, turn-of-the-century residence the zoning of which allowed for commercial uses. We strolled down to inspect his purchase. Along the way, we passed Casablanca House, a rabbit warren of offices where John Henshaw and Julian Grill were practising in partnership. Julian had been a contemporary of ours at Law School and was destined to become known many years later as a senior minister in the Burke and Dowding governments, a key figure in the chaotic era known as WA INC when various entrepreneurs, principally Alan Bond and Laurie Connell, plunged the government into some questionable business deals. For the moment, however, on his way past the Casablanca premises, Rob was chuffed to think that, once we moved into his newly acquired building, our firm would be the southernmost firm of solicitors in the city area: legalistic fringe-dwellers.

The building Rob had bought had previously been occupied by a firm of industrial chemists, Kavanagh and Inman. They had only just moved out. Cartons and heaps of cotton waste were all over the place, accompanied by a scattering of flasks and test tubes. We wandered through the debris and looked out the front window. Across the street we could see a ten-pin bowling alley. There was a used-car yard next door.

As we surveyed the wreckage around us, I asked Rob whether he had enough money to complete the deal.

He seemed surprised by the question. 'I'm working on it,' he said. 'There's plenty of time left to settlement. I'll scrape it up from somewhere.'

This appraisal of the situation, I learnt eventually, was typical of my new partner. He had a nerve of steel.

The settlement went through. The building was renovated. The space for parking out the back was much appreciated by our clients and business steadily improved. Rollo's business was improving too, which meant he was turning his agency's legal work my way.

His aim was to acquire tracts of land fit for subdivision into residential lots. They would be sold at a price sufficient to cover the costs of development and a margin for profit. The funds required to acquire the land and cover costs would be raised by forming a syndicate comprised principally of friends and acquaintances, with net profit to be shared according to the amount of capital contributed. I was to set the ball rolling by drafting a syndicate agreement and incorporating a company to manage the project: Hasluck and Morrison Projects Pty Ltd. Rollo's co-venturer, David Morrison, a registered builder, a friend of his from boating days, was agreeable to his name being included in the description of the new company.

I could have done without the diabolically complicated conveyancing work that came with the first tract of land they sought to acquire, some patches of bushland abutting Bilgoman Road at Glen Forrest in the Darling Range. An inhabitant of the main patch of land had sold it in the early 1950s to a storekeeper and his wife from Katanning, and they in turn had sold it to a couple of retired farmers from Koojan as tenants in common. In due course, one of these two assigned his interest to the other by a verbal contract on the basis that the assignee would discharge monies outstanding under the earlier contracts.

Rollo and I spent many a long hour on the veranda of the current inhabitant's bungalow on the bushland block while this tangled history was being sorted out. Rollo was at his best in a ticklish situation of this kind. He liked to talk, and always did so in a free and easy way. The farmer from Koojan liked Rollo's sense of humour, the style of someone who was prepared to buck the system, and proved helpful in tying up the loose ends from the earlier transactions.

We managed to get the necessary agreements and transfers signed eventually – documents to be executed by seven signatories in all. The other patches of land came with equally tangled histories. Rollo then had to obtain town planning approval as to the entirety in order to create an array of residential lots fronting a newly-constructed road called Glenwood Avenue, and with provision for public open space.

The development was called Glen Views Estate. The last bits and pieces of the jigsaw puzzle were finally fitted into place. A newsletter circulated to syndicate members by Hasluck and Morrison Projects provided this report:

> The subdivision of Glen Views Estate has now been completed and the vacant lots sold, without exception, for a price higher than that anticipated when the syndicate was formed in July 1968. No doubt all members of the syndicate will be pleased with the return. In this project we developed eight acres of land at Glen Forrest situated in an excellent position and for this reason were able to achieve maximum sale prices for the area on the twelve half-acre blocks offered to the public.

In the end, the development company's earnings by way of management fees and a share of the profit were somewhat less than the co-venturers had hoped for, bearing in mind the amount of time devoted to the project, but they had learnt some useful lessons along the way. More importantly perhaps, by the time the Glen Views Estate project was completed, they were pushing ahead with a number of other projects, employing the same model: syndicate and managing company.

All of this meant that, in addition to assembling evidence for use in court cases involving some of my other clients, I was spending a good deal of time assembling documents for Rollo and dealing with queries from a steadily expanding group of syndicate members, some of whom, as I cautioned Rollo, human nature being what it is, were inclined to nurse grievances if things didn't move quickly or go exactly according to plan.

For the time being, however, things were going well. To keep the narrative on a coherent track, I will skip over some of the difficulties the development company had to deal with while carrying into effect its other projects, and return to its newsletter for an overview.

> Planning for the Neerigen Heights Estate, as appears in our newsletter, is running ahead of schedule. Successful negotiations have been concluded with Page-Johnson Ltd, the large company owning land adjoining the syndicate's ten acres at Armadale. We now have a clear program outlined by them for the joint development of our two estates. As to the Fifth Road Estate it can now be said that the sub-division has been approved and there were no complicated conditions. We anticipate returning a dividend to subscribers within twelve months based on known costs and procedures.

The directors of Hasluck and Morrison Projects were minded also to draw upon the resources and experience of David Morrison's building firm. Their forward planning included the construction of a two-storey office building at 360 Rokeby Road, Subiaco, to be known as Yanderra House. This project, when completed, would give syndicate members a regular return from the rental. The company would occupy 25% of the office space available for itself and it had already pre-let a further 40% 'so we do not foresee any vacancy occurring'.

These business pursuits kept Rollo busy but he still found time for family activities and boating excursions on Freshwater Bay and to Rottnest. In October 1968, Jill gave birth to a son, Jeremy Hasluck, a welcome arrival who added another layer of well-being to life at Dartmouth Avenue.

In the meantime, however, although this was not known to those at Dartmouth Avenue or to the circle of family members and friends enjoying outings on Rollo's boat, moves were afoot in high places that would have a profound effect on my father's career.

In early January 1969, my parents left for London to attend a Commonwealth Prime Ministers Conference. Soon after they arrived, the Australian prime minister, John Gorton, had an audience with the Queen and asked her to approve Paul Hasluck as Governor-General of the Commonwealth of Australia, to which she assented.

The announcement was made a month later and my father then resigned from the House of Representatives as the member for Curtin – the seat he had held for twenty years. Arrangements were made for him to take up his new position at Government House in Canberra, in succession to Lord Casey, at the end of April. He was installed as a Knight Grand Cross of the Order of St Michael and St George during a visit to Windsor Castle.

In an interview in Perth shortly after these events, Paul said he was not entirely happy about leaving his home state but was looking forward to his term as Governor-General. 'At my advanced years,' he remarked' (he was sixty four) 'one does not become too excited.' My parents now had three grandchildren – Melissa, Anthony and Jeremy – and Sally was expecting a baby in August. Paul and Alix knew that vice-regal life would limit the time available for their role as grandparents.

The younger members of the family, Rollo and I especially, were certainly looking forward to what lay ahead. The first step in the new story would be a trip to Canberra for the swearing in of my father as Governor-General, and some related social functions at Government House, Yarralumla.

Government Houses

The media coverage of my father's appointment was favourable on the whole. An editorial in the *Sydney Morning Herald* reminded readers that 'a year ago the Herald supported Mr Hasluck's claim to be the leader of the Liberal Party and Prime Minister of Australia. We are glad to salute Sir Paul now as Australia's Governor-General.'

The *Sydney Sun*'s editorial was headed 'A Splendid Choice'. It went on to say, 'A distinguished Australian for Australia's most distinguished post.' It noted that the appointee 'comes straight from party politics and this can rightly be criticised. But he has ability that should enable him to fill the office of Governor-General and everyone must hope that he succeeds.'

The 'straight from politics' issue was picked up by some of the other papers including *The Age* of Melbourne. It said,

> Paul Hasluck's appointment is a controversial one. Critics will raise two arguments, one involving principles and the other personality. We doubt the validity of both arguments. Indeed it may well be that the qualities which have been liabilities during his political career will be assets in his new office.

The issue was taken further in some other reports which looked at appointees who had not only been active in public affairs but also had an Australian background. The first of them, Sir Isaac Isaacs, was Chief Justice of the High Court before his appointment in 1931. Sir William McKell was the Labor premier of New South Wales when he was appointed in 1947. Lord Casey, appointed in 1965, had served in the federal parliament for many years, and as a minister in the Menzies government, but was living in retirement when the announcement was made. It emerged, then, that Hasluck was the fourth Australian to be appointed as the Queen's representative under the Constitution but the first to be approved while serving in the federal parliament and as a minister.

Gallup Poll findings suggested, as the discussion ran on, that the general public wasn't greatly troubled by the issue. When sample groups throughout Australia were asked about the matter, 61% said they approved of Hasluck's appointment (approval reaching 75% in Western Australia), 17% disapproved and 22% were undecided. It seems that at the time of McKell's appointment, 38% approved but he gained approval as his term ran on, with the result that a Gallup Poll conducted towards the end of his term showed that 63% wanted him to continue in office.

All of those appointed in the decades following my father's term as Governor-General were Australian, including Bill Hayden, a federal parliamentarian who was serving as a Labor foreign minister at the time of his appointment. Discussion about the suitability of candidates has now moved on to look at gender and identity issues and, increasingly, with debate about an Australian head of state, under a republican constitution perhaps, hovering in the background. But fifty years ago, in 1969, the principal issue was whether Lord Casey would be succeeded by another Australian.

The 'straight from politics' issue was a real issue, but within a few weeks, the debate petered out, probably for the reason given by editorial in *The Age*. Photographs of the appointee's family appeared in the press. Paul was kept busy responding to the flood of congratulatory telegrams and letters and making arrangements for the move to Government House at Yarralumla.

The arrangements included provision for family members to attend the swearing-in ceremony to be held at Parliament House in Canberra at the end of April, so Rollo and I combined to engage a domestic help with experience in caring for young children to join us on the trip. In that way, our children – Melissa, Anthony and Jeremy – would be properly looked after as the formalities and related social functions took place. The diary I kept at that time includes a graphic account of what we saw and did.

Tues 29 April. The children's carer, Sue Harkness, arrives. We board the official cars a little later, at about 9 a.m., with Sally and I in one car and Sue and Anthony in the car ahead. On our way to the airport, while crossing the causeway, we see Jill and her parents in another car. Upon arrival at the airport we are told that Jill's sister, Jocelyn, has just given birth to a daughter, which is pleasing. While we are waiting for the rest of the group to assemble, a reporter approaches me in a friendly way and asks whether Lord Casey, the outgoing Governor-General, will greet us in Canberra. I mention a report in her own paper to the effect that Lord Casey flew out of Canberra yesterday.

My parents, PH and AH, are waiting on the tarmac by the RAAF aircraft. Press photographers take some informal photos of our group as we are milling about on our way to the plane. When a picture appears on the front page of the *Daily News* that afternoon, it shows me, to my embarrassment, on the edge of the group in horn-rimmed spectacles, bearing a black briefcase and a furled umbrella, as though I'm off to a meeting of highly-priced legal eagles.

The interior of the VIP plane is comfortable indeed. Melissa and Anthony run up and down the aisle shouting and chortling, while baby Jeremy looks on. When we strap ourselves in before taking off the children are mystified. Why the big belts?

I chat to AH about her recent trip to England and her visit to Windsor Castle. It seems that she and PH were housed in the Lancaster Tower whose windows overlook the Long Walk to the equestrian statue of George III in the distance. At about 6 p.m. they were conducted to the Green Drawing Room where Paul was dubbed GCMG by the Queen. This was followed by dinner and a visit to the Library to see some royal treasures. These included the linen shirt worn by King Charles I at his execution in the aftermath of the Civil War. During our chat Paul produces the decoration he received. This will be worn when he is sworn in as GG tomorrow. Alix goes on to describe her dinner at the Savoy Hotel a few days later with Sally's parents, Robert and Irene Bolton, who had come from their home in the Cotswolds for the occasion.

We read for a while as the flight proceeds, then Sally and I adjourn to the back of the plane for lunch with my father's Protocol Officer, Geoffrey Pretyman, and the naval aide-de-camp, Lieutenant Blackband. As we chat Pretyman describes how he was taken prisoner in Africa during the war years. The young Lieutenant chips in at the end of the story: 'I suppose you must have been rather ashamed of yourself.' Which was not exactly a tactful remark.

On the approach to Canberra PH and AH change into formal attire. We pass over the Cotter River and catch a first glimpse of Government House at Yarralumla – a cluster of buildings on the edge of Lake Burley Griffin. When the plane lands – at 4 p.m. precisely, per the schedule – my parents descend. The rest of us, still aboard, watch from windows of the plane. PH in a black homburg hat is a greeted by the Prime Minister, John Gorton, and various other dignitaries including the President of the Senate, the Speaker, the Deputy Prime Minister (John McEwen) and the Leader of the Opposition (Gough Whitlam). Accompanied by the Guard Commander and the duty aide-de-camp, PH then inspects a Guard of Honour lined up on the tarmac.

We leave the plane once the formalities are over and are taken to some waiting cars. Sally and I board one of these with Miss Susan Hewitt, who was a personal assistant to Lady Casey and will serve as such with my mother. The convoy of cars with a motor cycle escort in front surges through Canberra to Yarralumla. It is my first time back in Canberra for six years or so. The newly-created lake adds to the beauty of the city but seems artificial, as compared with the former grassy flats and meandering course of the Molonglo River, flanked here and there by languid willow trees. It is reassuring to notice that the cutting for the road leading from Capital Hill to Commonwealth Avenue remains roughly-hewn stone, essentially unaltered.

We sweep down the foliage-laded Dunrossil Avenue on the approach to Government House, the trees golden in the autumn light. Beneath the portico at the front entrance we are introduced to the Official Secretary, Sir Murray Tyrell, and various members of the household staff. We are taken upstairs and shown our bedrooms which, in our case, form part of the VIP suite: Rollo and Jill to the left of the central corridor; Nick and Sally to the right. The corridor leads to a comfortable living room with a magnificent view of the distant Uriarra mountain range.

We come down for tea. Blackband, still on duty as aide-de-camp, offers me a sticky bun, for which I thank him, but am left with sticky fingers and nowhere to put it. Rollo and I are introduced to Paul Mench, the military aide-de-camp and to Commander Warren Brash, the Military Secretary to the Governor-General. Rollo and I glance at each other. We foresee difficulties in remembering all these names and positions.

After tea, Rollo and I stroll around the grounds with PH and out to the little peninsula by the Lake. There is a familiar crispness, a degree of chill, in the Canberra air. Across the lake, the golden trees of autumn are reflected on the surface of the tranquil water. Now, at last, with my briefcase confined to the wardrobe, I begin to feel that I am on holiday.

We stroll on past an enclosure for kangaroos. PH says that he disapproves of this, and will do something about it. We walk on to the drive and to an area known as the 'wild garden'. Here, surrounded by foliage at the end of a winding path, we find the statuette of a solitary boy in the centre of a pond. The lip of the pond bears an inscription: 'To Pat's Youth and Happy Hours'. This, it seems, was erected to commemorate a child of Lord and Lady Gowrie, a former vice-regal couple, whose much-loved only son was killed near Tripoli during the war.

In the main house again, after our visit to the Gowrie 'wild garden', we join Jill and Sally upstairs and dress for dinner. We descend to a drinks trolley manned by an aide-de-camp. I am handed a pre-dinner martini. It is a black tie dinner and, as if to emphasise that this is Government House, a vice-regal world with its own conventions, Paul Mench, in military uniform, shows each of us the seating plan before we cross the hall to the dining room.

I am placed next to Mrs Thompson, the wife of the assistant to Sir Murray Tyrell. The latter is across from me, a tall, heavily bespectacled, almost Edwardian figure, with dark hair slicked neatly into place. On my left is Miss Sue Hewitt. She describes her days as personal secretary to a travel agent in London. She was also secretary to Lady Rachel Cleland, wife of the Administrator in Papua New Guinea during my father's time as Minister for Territories. Fortunately, this gives me something to talk about because I met Rachel Cleland on various occasions while travelling in PNG. I am told that, in retirement, the Clelands have stayed on in New Guinea.

We adjourn to the main lounge room after dinner. I am placed beside Mrs Tyrell and on this occasion also it turns out that there are things to talk about. She describes the courtship of her daughter Margot by George Martin, my former teammate from debating days at Canberra Grammar School: an early engagement was broken off at one stage, but followed by marriage eventually.

I have an impression, as I glance at the conversations going on around me, that the members of staff including Commander Brash, the aides-de-camp and the elderly Pat Roderiguez – the Comptroller of the House – would like the newcomers to head upstairs to their rooms so that those who remain can settle down to a nightcap and a leisurely chat. But Rollo is firmly entrenched, waxing lyrical about the pros and cons of real estate, the ups and downs of the market, and so on.

When our parents leave, Rollo calls for beer. Surprise! Is beer unmentionable? Not so, apparently. We stay for a quick one. Then off to bed, although, for us, who started the day in west coast time, it is still early. Not yet ready for bed, I sit in the lounge room for a while, beneath a landscape by Arthur Streeton, and thumb through some books on Government House.

Government House, Canberra, was built in 1897 and was therefore created after the more imposing vice-regal residences in the various states of Australia. It was created essentially as a comfortable country house situated on what was once a large sheep station of 39,000 acres.

The House began as a tall gabled building of three storeys in height. When Canberra was founded as the Federal Capital the house and land were acquired by the government for a vice-regal residence, and various alterations and additions were made, including the construction of a two-storeyed wing with a huge drawing-room, a dining room and a study on the ground floor. A commodious VIP suite of rooms was created on the second storey, and numerous bedrooms with bathrooms attached. Most of the pictures on the walls, including the Streeton landscape in this room presumably, are on loan from and belong to the National Gallery.

I return the books to the shelf beside me, conscious that the time has come to turn in. We have a big day ahead of us tomorrow.

*

Wed 30 April. I wake at 7.40 a.m. Dress quickly to be at breakfast with Rollo and PH. in the living room of our suite. We sit by the broad front window. A morning of heavy mist out there on the lawns of Government House. On a stroll with Sally afterwards we encounter Rollo and PH by the kangaroo enclosure. Then PH slips off to be 'briefed' about the forthcoming ceremony. He is to be sworn in as Governor-General at 11 a.m. in the Senate Chamber.

We go inside to change and at 10.50 a.m. on the dot, as stipulated on the daily program, or briefing sheet – we are becoming used to sheets of this kind – we are dutifully waiting under the portico to be collected by official cars. Everything has to run like clockwork, we are led to believe, otherwise there will be chaos and confusion.

We enjoy the drive to Parliament House, for it is now a bright sunny day. There is a crowd of bystanders on the front steps, the War Memorial in the distance. We are met by Peter Harvey from the Prime Minister's Department and taken up to King's Hall. There, surrounded by official portraits of former Prime Ministers and other luminaries, we are approached by journalists and positioned for photographs – Rollo, Jill, Sally and myself, doing our best to look alert, at ease in these surroundings.

We are led to a seat inside the Senate Chamber. The huge room with its crimson seats begins to fill with parliamentarians, and the galleries overhead are becoming crowded too. Arthur Calwell, the former Leader of the Opposition comes in, limping slightly. Then the judiciary in their wigs and gowns. How tired and careworn, they seem, these elderly faces beneath their wigs. The Chief Justice, Sir Garfield Barwick, casually tosses an old-fashioned tri-corn hat on the central table as he moves to his place: a tradition of some kind, I presume. The Prime Minister, John Gorton and his wife Bettina Gorton, take a seat on a dais by the Senate President's Chair. Alix looks on from a seat nearby, wearing an elegant strawberry pink jacket suit and a black velvet beret.

The Official Party arrives led by Black Rod in traditional costume, knee-breeches and with a white jabot for a collar. PH takes his place at the centre of the Chamber and requests all present to be seated. The Chief Justice of the High Court, Sir Garfield Barwick administers the oath of office. That done, Tyrell, the Official Secretary, speaks loudly into the microphone: 'God Save the Queen.' On cue, a gun booms in the distance. I presumed that this occurred because everything has been so beautifully timed pursuant to the clockwork credo, with all the watches in and around the building being synchronised. But I am told later that the gunners were in fact responding to a signalling device.

The ceremony over, we leave the Senate Chamber. More photographs, and we are then conducted to an ante chamber adjoining the hall where the official reception is to be held. We are introduced to the PM's daughter, Joanna Gorton. We chat briefly to our parents as the dignitaries arrives. We attach ourselves to the end of the line and move on to join the throng within. We meet the Canadian Ambassador and his wife, the Ghanaian Ambassador and his wife, Mrs Sekyi – both lively – and the New Zealanders, Mr and Mrs Hazlett. Rollo and I are pleased to have a chat with Lady Wheeler. She and her husband Fred Wheeler, the Treasury Secretary, are known to us from our years in Canberra during the war, for we were friends with their children – Pam, Elizabeth and Philip Wheeler. It seems that Philip will soon be on his way to Oxford.

Rollo and I are then accosted by my father's close friend, Fred Chaney, MHR for Perth. In his usual jocular way Fred invites us to join the 'larrikins' at the bar. We do so. Sir Garfield Barwick strides briskly across to join the group. This leads to some badinage about his time in parliament before his appointment to the High Court. Fred presses Barwick as to whether he spotted the row of 'defrocked priests' in the Senate Chamber – Fred Chaney, Don Chipp et cetera. I take this to be a reference to certain ministers who lost their portfolios in a recent reshuffle. I am aware that Fred's term as Minister for Navy, unfortunately, was clouded by the Voyager controversy; Chipp was formerly a Minister for Customs.

We are gathered up after a while by our escort from the PM's department and taken back to King's Hall. Some more photographs of the younger Haslucks. That done, we follow the official party down the steps leading to the entrance, then to the sunlit landing out front where PH takes the salute from an array of uniforms on the lawn below: the formal guard. While gazing at the distant War Memorial I wonder whether lofty thoughts would be appropriate, but I abandon the attempt as they don't seem to come. PH inspects the guard and is ushered to the waiting car. Somewhere near me an official hisses to the crowd around the front steps: 'You may cheer if you wish.' Desultory clapping. We are escorted to our own car and driven away.

*

After lunch in the dining room at Government House Rollo and I go across to my father's flat at 60 Macgregor Street to pick up my father's Peugeot. Enough to remind us of our trip across the Nullarbor in the old green Peugeot so many years ago. But this model, the replacement, is a beige-coloured station wagon, and possibly more durable. We gather up some other items from the flat with a degree of regret, realising that this is the last we will see of our former weekend refuge from the boarding house at school.

Back at Yarralumla, with our own private transport now, we pick up PH and the girls and drive to Mrs Llewellyn's stables nearby, just off the Cotter Road. PH has kept various horses here over a number of years. He takes us to an inner yard to meet his pal, Mrs Llewellyn, the owner of the stables and a related Riding School. She is anxious about PH going for a ride right now because his horse hasn't been exercised for a while and seems restive. He overrules her objection, so we leave him there to saddle up. The four of us drive to the Red Hill Lookout overlooking Canberra. We admire the view, descend to Mugga Way, cruise past a line of embassies and the front oval of Canberra Grammar School, and finish up at the Manuka shopping centre. Here, Rollo and I dash into a shop to buy dress shirts to go with our tuxedos.

We head back to the stables and on the way there, not far from Government House, we see the newly-appointed Governor-General to one side of the busy road, astride his trusty mount. We return to Government House eventually for a cup of tea, and to join Sue Harkness for playtime with Melissa and Anthony. Sir Murray Tyrell arrives to inform PH that one of the guests tonight, the President of the Senate, will be bringing a Bill for signature. Tyrell begins to instruct PH in matters of procedure. At the end of the explanation, PH asks what the Bill is about. Tyrell replies: 'Good heavens, I don't know.' This was not the response PH was looking for, and I can see he is displeased.

The four of us in the VIP suite – Jill, Rollo, Sally and I – assemble briefly in our lounge room to ensure that we are all properly fitted out for the part we have to play. We descend. Sir Garfield Barwick and his wife arrive, the Gortons soon afterwards. I am seated next to Lady Barwick, just across from the PM with his familiar craggy face. I understand from the write ups that Gorton was injured in an air crash during the war, but his injuries have certainly left with him a dashing, rugged look. Having quizzed me briefly about my career in the law to date, he tells me that his lawyer son is going to the Bar in Melbourne tomorrow. 'It will be the end of a safe life as a solicitor,' Gorton says, 'but who wants to be safe. The Bar is the place to go. If a lawyer is any good he will succeed. If he fails, then that's the way it ought to be. The only problem with that approach is if a man gets ill.'

It seems the PM is due to leave for America in coming days, so those around him ask about the trip. He makes light of the busy days ahead and says only that the official party will be hoping to get some rest on the way back. This prompts him to come up with a little story about what lies ahead in parliament. The best parliament would be one that never assembles, he jokes. The elected members could simply press a switch to vote. It would save the inconvenience of attending parliament and that would, of course, suit a lot of those presently obliged to attend.

These remarks seem typical of the PM, consistent with what was said about him during the leadership contest twelve months ago. There is a kind of couldn't-care-less disregard for the usual niceties in his tone, a desire to shock, an assertiveness, all which are probably attractive qualities in an old soldier or a club man surrounded by a group of friends, but seem slightly out of place coming from a Prime Minister in a formal dining room. I initiate a discussion about the new Hancock and Wright newspaper, The Independent, which has just got under way in the West. Gorton says that he met the two mining men in Perth recently. He points out, dismissively, that they both have a 19th century laissez faire attitude to the economy, but he doesn't elaborate.

The ladies retire to the living room which prompts PH to rearrange the seating for those remaining at the dinner table. He invites me to sit next to Barwick with the gambit: 'This is the only lawyer in the Hasluck family.' Barwick smiles wanly. Some badinage about lawyers prompts him to say, as if to illustrate the transience of legal careers, that on one occasion, when he took a matter to the Privy Council in London, the applicant died before the matter was brought on for hearing.

After a while we rise and join the ladies for coffee. Jill and I sit with Mrs Gorton. She is an American who met her husband during his undergraduate days at Oxford. She mentions a recent trip to the United States. This included an excursion to Maine, in a special jet provided by President Lyndon Johnson, although they were there for only a few hours. In response to some remarks she has made about living in the Prime Minister's Lodge, I say that in my school days certain boys in the district were in the habit of getting autographs from the guards at the front gate. Mrs Gorton is a fairly serious woman and doesn't seem to find this tale amusing, so I change the subject.

An aide-de-camp, quietly and efficiently, is shifting people about, so I find myself, again, with PH and Barwick, engaged in further talk about the law. PH mentions that while in London recently he visited Ede and Ravenscroft, the legal outfitters in Chancery Lane – to pick up the wig I ordered upon admission to the Bar in Perth not so long ago. Barwick says that the wig he wore for the swearing-in ceremony in the Senate Chamber earlier in the day belonged to a former High Court Judge, Sir George Rich, and is therefore both old and venerable.

The time comes for PH and AH, now the vice-regal couple, to take their leave, and this is done in accordance with what seems to be the usual protocol. A line is formed as they bid farewell to the various guests. The men bow; the women curtsy. As the room clears, Jill and Sally go upstairs, leaving Rollo and me to have a nightcap with the duty aides-de-camp, Paul Mench and Peter Blackband. We talk about the Jervis Bay Naval College at Nowra and our excursion on crash boats after playing rugby there some years ago. We finish up talking about military strategy and the capability of nuclear weapons. To bed eventually.

*

The newspapers next morning covered the swearing-in ceremony in detail. The various reports added an extra layer to the account presented in my diary, so I will draw upon them to round out the story of what took place.

According to one paper, with Sir Paul Hasluck installed yesterday as Australia's seventeenth Governor-General, 'the pattern of appointing a distinguished Australian to the post should now be irrevocably established'. The brief solemn ceremony was said to have been carried out in the Senate chamber. The oaths of allegiance and of office were administered by the Chief Justice of the High Court in a chamber crowded with members of both houses, diplomats, service chiefs, former ministers and departmental heads.

In the course of the proceedings, according to another report, the Chief Justice, Sir Garfield Barwick, caused concern among parliamentary circles by laying his three-cornered hat and his gloves on the Senate chamber before the swearing in of the Governor-General. There is a tradition that this is an indication of defiance of parliament. The President of the Senate, Sir Alister McMullen, set the record straight. The Senate was not assembled as a Senate at the time, he said. Sir Garfield was following another tradition. When the Chief Justice places his hat and gloves on the table, it indicates independence of the judiciary from the Crown.

It emerges from the press reports that the gathering of parliamentarians and dignitaries overflowed into the public galleries. Some MPs watched the ceremony on TV in King's Hall. The Leader of the Opposition, Mr Whitlam, and senior ministers Fairhall, Anthony, Sinclair, Fraser and Barnes sat in the front bench Opposition seats. On the other side of the chamber were the treasurer Mr McMahon and the deputy prime minister McEwen with their wives.

A sudden hush came over the crowd as the Usher of the Black Rod appeared. Sir Paul, looking immaculate in morning suit, moved to the President's seat. All eyes were on him.

In taking the oath Sir Paul swore, 'I will well and truly serve in the office of Governor-General in the Commonwealth...and do right by all manner of people within the laws, without fear or favour, affection or ill-will.' Sir Murray Tyrell, secretary to governors-general for twenty-two years read the proclamation empowering Sir Paul 'with all the powers, rights, grants and privileges of the office.' It was signed Elizabeth R and countersigned J.G. Gorton.

As the official secretary ended his reading of the proclamation with the words 'God Save the Queen', the first round of a twenty-one-gun salute was fired by a battery from the Royal Military College on the lawns in front of Parliament House. At the reception later, guests were presented to Sir Paul and Lady Hasluck.

I must now return to my diary.

Thurs 1 May. Up at 7 a.m. to join PH and Rollo for breakfast in the front room of our suite. After reading the press coverage of yesterday's ceremony, Sally and I join Rollo and Jill downstairs by the Peugeot. We drive to Parliament House for Question Time in the House of Representatives. Green benches. We sit in a ground floor gallery, behind Victor Garland, who has taken over from PH as the member for Curtin. The questions put to the Prime Minister seem fairly tame. John Gorton, in the Prime Minister's seat at the central table, disposes of them easily, sometimes with a dash of laconic humour.

From Parliament House we cross the Lake to visit the shopping complex at Civic Centre for coffee. And for Rollo and I to buy some tennis shorts. The aides-de-camp have challenged us to a game of squash, and also to tennis on the courts at Government House. We buy some theatre tickets and stop to have our personalities analysed by a new-fangled computer set up in one of the shopping arcades. It seems from the print out that the best professions and hobbies for me are: 'Display artist, decoration, illumination, interior decorator, composer, carpenter, string musician, paper manufacturer, radio and television artist, commercial agent, lawyer, librarian, teacher, agriculture work.' The machine presents Rollo and the others with some equally bizarre analyses. If this is the best computers can do the future looks uncertain. But things will probably run on as before.

We return to Government House for lunch. This is followed,

for Rollo and me at least, kitted out in our new shorts, by a trip to squash courts near Manuka. We work up a sweat with Paul Mench and Commander Brash. Our theatre tickets take us back to Civic Centre in the evening for a production of *The Boys in the Band* about a group of gay friends in New York. In the row behind us we are pleased to chance upon our long-standing Canberra friend from earlier days, Philip Wheeler, and a friend of his Margaret Cobb. The play over, we are invited back to Philip's home near Red Hill for a nightcap. We offer Margaret a lift home to the Girls' Grammar School in Melbourne Avenue where she is a resident teacher in the boarding house.

*

Fri 2 May. A visit to the National Library where we are shown round by my parents' friend from the war years, Pauline Fanning. We chance upon the West Australian academic Brian de Garis, a well-known historian. We are introduced to the ANU poet and Professor of Literature, Bob Brissenden. Back to Yarralumla for lunch. Another trip to the squash court with Commander Brash for Rollo and me.

*

Sat 3 May. We take the kids to the War Memorial. Rollo and I are at a loose end after lunch so we go to an Australian rules football match at Manuka oval. It is cold, and the standard of play is appalling. So we leave. We drive up Flinders Way to the oval at Canberra Grammar School looking for a rugby match. But there is none. We finish up watching a game at the Duntroon military college out near the airport. I can feel a sore throat coming on.

We dress for dinner, feeling slightly nervous, as we, the four younger Haslucks, are the guests of honour on this occasion – my parents have arranged a dinner party for guests mainly of our own age. We see from the guest list that some of our suggestions have been taken up with the result that a number of the guests are known to us. On the list from school days in Canberra Grammar are Philip Wheeler, George Martin, Angus Moir, Peter Ewens.

Those known to us, as migrants to Canberra from the West, are John Foreman, Rosemary Mayne-Wilson and David Knapp (a veteran, or should I say survivor, of Chez Rollo days in the playroom at 2 Adams Road, but now installed in the Territories Department). We notice also Jill Paterson (a cousin from Queensland) and Murray Tyrell's daughters Leonie and Margot.

Rollo, Jill, Sally and I line up by the front door as cars begin to pull up at the front entrance, beneath the portico. We greet those we know and an aide-de-camp is there with a list to introduce us to the others. A pre-dinner drink before moving to the dining room. I am seated next to Mrs Geoffrey White, the wife of a youngish diplomat from the External Affairs Department. The dining table is a beautiful sight, stretching the length of the room, scintillating with crystal and silver, crisp white serviettes along the way. I chat briefly to David Knapp and to my cousin from Queensland, Jill Paterson, near me at the table.

The carpet in the lounge room has been pulled back to allow for dancing. Rollo has run for cover so I find myself being urged by the aides to help get things under way. Rosemary Mayne-Wilson (formerly Rosemary Thomas), recently recruited to External Affairs, was in my circle some years ago on the UWA campus so I persuade her to join me on the floor. Her first diplomatic posting was to South Africa, she tells me, and she now has two children. We are soon surrounded by a number of dancers. When the music stops I slip away for a chat with my former debating teammate, George Martin, and am updated about mutual friends from Canberra school days. Heather Sutherland is in America doing a PhD in oriental studies. Noel Pratt is a journalist with *The Australian*. George himself has embarked on a law degree, and aspires to win a seat for the Labor Party in the federal parliament.

We are joined by Philip Wheeler. I ask if it is possible to go through the ANU these days without emerging as a radical. Philip says yes, but George hesitates. In the early sixties, he says, the staff with their radical views were closer to the students and his answer might have been no. But things may have changed since then. The conversation is getting interesting when AH appears at my elbow, disengages me from the group, and invites me to meet Virginia Wilton, daughter of General Sir John Wilton.

From the daughter of a General to Angus Moir, son of a local architect. Angus is presently running a pottery in Paddington but is still hoping to complete a degree in architecture at Sydney University. He updates me on some others known to Rollo and me from school days. Tony Voutas dropped out of the ANU, went to New Guinea as a patrol officer, and now, as a member of the PNG parliament, he is playing a key role in the PANGU party's push for independence. Bob Sorby and Paul Murphy are in the Canberra press gallery. David Oliphant is or will soon be a priest. Our former English teacher, the Reverend Jack Tyrell, is seeking to start a school of his own. I notice, in a corner of my eye, that AH has appeared at Rollo's elbow and is moving him purposefully towards some other group.

The dancing ends and we say goodbye to them all eventually, pleased that our party has gone so well.

*

Sun 4 May. My sore throat isn't any better. Worse, in fact. After lunch we drive to a polo match in a paddock on the outskirts of Canberra. Sally and I are looked after by a woman called Dinny Killen. She is quiet and serene which means I can talk to her without straining my afflicted vocal chords. We confess to knowing nothing about polo and this seems to please her. She went to Frensham, the well-known girls' school near Mittagong, and is here in the paddock, it seems, at her husband's insistence, although I can't quite gather whether he is a player or simply an enthusiastic supporter. PH and AH are called upon to present trophies when the game ends.

Back to Yarralumla for supper. The Butler, Bryan George, hands me a hot lemon drink to soothe the aching throat. And so to bed.

*

Mon 5 May. We board the Peugeot and set off for Sydney along Northbourne Avenue: Rollo and Jill in the front seat, Sally and I behind. We reach the foreshore of Lake George, pass through Goulburn, and stop for lunch eventually at a pleasant little inn outside

Camden. We are soon fighting our way through Sydney traffic to reach the Belvedere Hotel at Kings Cross where Rollo and Jill stayed some years ago in the course of their honeymoon. We cross Sydney Harbour Bridge in the early evening and find our way to an old time Music Hall in Military Road at Neutral Bay. We take in a melodrama called *O Vile Pretender*, enriched by bad jokes and pratfalls, overrun by the antics of implausible villains and equally implausible virgins. Back at the hotel, some coffee keeps us up long enough to take a closer look at our surroundings.

*

The Belvedere was a stately home which was commandeered for official purposes during World War II. It then became a private hotel with a fine dining room and a reputation for French cuisine. A good deal of its original character remained. At the time of our stay, it was still a gracious old white-painted Victorian mansion with wisteria-twined balconies and shady courtyard, camphor laurels and marble statues, a splendid fountain. It stood in an acre of gardens among Moreton Bay fig trees, palms and creamy-flowered magnolias. The interior included rooms enhanced by chandeliers and Persian rugs. The atmosphere was New Orleans belle époque and the hotel's personal service was in keeping with the traditions of the grand old European hotels. In its heyday after the war it was, in the opinion of its regular patrons, an enclave of solitude and old world values that refused to capitulate to the demands of progress.

Unfortunately, at the time of our stay, and this could be gleaned from the conversations going on around us and from what was said at the desk when we arrived, it seemed that the Belvedere's days were numbered. The hotel and its grounds had been resumed by the Department of Main Roads and were destined to be demolished in order to make way for the Kings Cross tunnel adjoining Bayswater Road. Not surprisingly, the hotel's facade and splendid interior were affected to some extent by a mood of melancholy, the knowledge that the style these architectural features represented would soon be coming to an end. It was to have no place in the future of Kings Cross and Rushcutters Bay.

This was sad, but made us even more determined to enjoy our brief sojourn at this place, and in Sydney generally. As my diary shows.

*

Tues 6 May. Breakfast at the hotel is followed by a shopping expedition to Double Bay. Rollo and Jill stay on, while Sally and I go off to have lunch at the Weinkeller restaurant in Pitt Street, a place recommended by Sue Harkness for its German menu and atmosphere. We browse in the Angus and Robertson bookshop, then in David Jones by Hyde Park. Back to the hotel for a rest. Dinner at a Chinese restaurant in Dixon Street followed by a movie at a nearby cinema: *The Shoes of the Fisherman* based on the novel by Australian author Morris West. We walk back to Kings Cross in the rain.

*

Wed 7 May. The four of us go on a drive to the North Shore, then on to Church Point and Palm Beach. In the evening we find our way to a flat occupied by two business friends of Rollo, one of whom, I understand, is an assistant manager of a prominent restaurant near Circular Quay. The other fellow is a rather flashy TV type, brimful of anecdotes about celebrities and so on. We have some drinks for a while, with Rollo and the two local boys doing most of the talking. Then, as the conversation doesn't seem to be going anywhere in particular, they take us to a strip show in Kings Cross. From there we move on to swell the crowd at Les Girls, where an array of female impersonators are strutting their stuff in gorgeous costumes and feathered headdresses. We are expected to applaud, and do so. Back to the Belvedere by midnight. Rollo is full of praise for his friends, a 'pair of live wires' et cetera, but I am not so sure. To me, they seem a bit too full of themselves.

*

Thurs 8 May. To Paddington where we visit the Kim Bonython art gallery and my friend Angus Moir's pottery. Then back to the Belvedere for lunch beside the exquisite courtyard. After lunch, as previously arranged, we drive across the Harbour Bridge to Kirribilli for a visit to Admiralty House, a chance to wander around the vice-regal premises and to take in the view from Kirribilli Point of the still-to-be-completed Sydney Opera House and the ferry stations at Circular Quay.

We talk our way past the guard at the front gate, citing the previously made arrangements, and find our way to the Comptroller of the House at the front door. He takes us from room to room, provides an overview of the place and its earlier history, then leaves us to poke about as we please. There don't seem to be any other staff members about, which gives the place a deserted feeling.

Admiralty House, it seems, was acquired by the Commander-in-Chief of her Majesty's ships when Sydney became the principal naval depot in the South Seas. Sixteen years later, after Federation, it was lent to the Commonwealth government as a Sydney residence for the Governor-General, and eventually became Commonwealth property. Floodlit at night, clearly visible to ferry passengers on the waters of the harbour, the residence's sandstone walls and arcaded verandas rise above and overshadow the less imposing premises nearby known as Kirribilli House – the Prime Minister's Sydney dwelling.

Inside Admiralty House, on the ground floor, one is immediately confronted by a magnificent staircase. The long flight of steps draws the observer's eye upwards to stained glass panels featuring the crests of past admirals who served in Sydney, and to some colourful coats of arms. The drawing room adjacent to the staircase overlooks the main lawn and the harbour, as do the adjoining dining room and the Governor-General's study further on. We notice, here and there, pictures by well-known Australian artists, such as Fred Williams and Sydney Nolan, for it seems that Lord Casey and his wife favoured contemporary works.

Outside again, we wander down the expansive lawn to cliffs above the rocky foreshore. From here a fine view is provided of the old mid-harbour prison called affectionately, despite its grim history, 'Pinchgut'. Below the cliffs, we find our way down to a tranquil outdoor swimming pool, partly sheltered from the wind by high, ivy-covered walls. It is here that the incorrigible Rollo manages to uplift a circular life-saving float from one of the railings, bearing the inscription 'Admiralty House – Kirribilli'. He creates a rounded frame for his smiling face. Flanked by Jill and Sally, I take a photo that is bound to become (in Rollo's opinion at least) an iconic image to mark our visit to this place. The arc of the Harbour Bridge will be faintly visible in the background.

We leave the life-saver buoy in its proper place, return to our car, say our farewells to the Comptroller of the House, and drive away. A little later, we have a quick bite to eat at small restaurant in Kings Cross called the 'Salad Bowl' (recommended by my friend from school days, Angus Moir) and go on to the Parade Theatre in Kensington. Here we attend a production of Tom Stoppard's play *Rosencratz and Guildenstern are Dead*.

The Stoppard play is a surrealistic farce, enriched by ingenious word play. It is certainly of a far higher order than the *Vile Pretender* play we saw at the old time music hall a few nights ago.

Tonight's play tracks the misadventures of two feckless friends from Hamlet's schooldays. They are unexpectedly summoned to Elsinore castle to provide some sort of advice about the Prince of Denmark's peculiar mental condition. They wander through the corridors of power with a group of itinerant players, apprehensive and bewildered, confused by fruitless discussions about time and chance ('death: the absence of presence'), but without knowing anything much about the political skulduggery swirling around them or the nature of their assignment. They die at sea eventually while taking Hamlet to England on a mission that is not quite clear to them. Amidst all the confusion, their only consolation is a thought voiced by one of the players: 'Every exit is an entrance somewhere else.'

On the way back to the Belvedere Hotel, our unusual belle époque sanctuary, we can't help wondering whether the surrealistic tale we have just enjoyed is a reflection of our own adventures in recent days: a summons to Canberra, jostled about by photographers in King's Hall, hustled into the red Senate chamber for a swearing-in ceremony, bustled into a green chamber for Question Time, wandering in and out of various government houses, mesmerised in the end by a glimpse of Pinchgut prison and a half-finished Opera House. Yes, a phantasmagoria of improbable images. Something to sleep on, at the very least.

*

Fri. 9 May. We drive Rollo and Jill to the airport. The idea is that Sally and I will keep the Peugeot wagon for the time being, stay on in Sydney for a few extra days, and then drive north to explore the Hawkesbury River and some inland centres before returning to Canberra.

Back to Business

Our trip to Canberra for the swearing-in ceremony and related events was enjoyable but a far cry from our usual round. The time had come to get back to Perth – to reality. This included, unfortunately, dealing with an unexpected legal issue that had arisen towards the end of our sojourn in the east. Our cheerful domestic companion, Sue Harkness, a friend to all of us by now, was injured in a traffic accident while staying at Government House.

It happened like this. Sue was on her way to the shopping precinct at Kingston in a Commonwealth car, seated beside the driver, when the car was struck by an oncoming vehicle. It was a relief to learn that Melissa and Anthony weren't with her when the accident happened, but a matter of deep distress that she was injured in this way, and would have to endure an operation, perhaps several operations, for the mending of her hip and leg.

Her medical expenses and consequential loss were fully covered in due course when it was established that the other driver was liable. In the meantime, however, help was at hand from another quarter. I had taken out an insurance policy before we left for Canberra, more by chance than by conscientious forward planning, I have to confess. The insurance office was in the same building as the Married Persons Summary Relief Court, so I had time enough to fill in the insurance forms while waiting for one of my cases to be called on. This insurance cover meant that in the period before fault was admitted by the other driver, Rollo and I could insist that Sue be provided for. I am pleased to say that in the end she made a full recovery. Nonetheless, in the days following our return from Canberra, the negotiations concerning the claim were a reminder that our halcyon holiday had come to an end – we were back to our daily round in Perth and, in Rollo's case, back to business.

In addition to managing his previously established syndicates and completing the office block in Subiaco known as Yanderra House, Rollo had other ideas afoot. He and David Morrison were finalising plans for a second office block in Rokeby Road, to be called Bindarra House. Hasluck and Morrison Projects Pty Ltd were planning also another subdivisional development at a site adjoining Postans Road in Cockburn to be known as Cockburn Gardens Residential Estate. The brochure for their proposal was persuasive:

> The land is currently zoned rural but is expected to be re-zoned Urban in the not too distant future. It is lightly timbered with good sandy soil and is close to the existing urban centres of Medina and the more recently developed Deepdene Estate. The future of this area is assured due to its position close to the Kwinana Industrial Complex and also to the main Fremantle– Rockingham Road.

Rollo was also working with an entrepreneurial group to acquire and develop a tract of bushland on the south coast of Western Australia to the west of Albany, near the township of Denmark. The proposed development would be known as Palos Verdes Estates and would involve the construction of a new road to the tip of the Nullaki Peninsula, where the Denmark river entered the sea. This would be followed by the creation of large bush blocks, several acres or more, which would probably be attractive to recreational fishermen as a base from which to embark upon fishing trips in the Southern Ocean or along the sparsely inhabited coastline to the Walpole Inlet and other secluded sites.

With another group of local businessmen, some with previous experience of working in Bali and Sumatra, Rollo was looking for business opportunities in Indonesia. The memorandum of understanding I prepared for the group included this very confident assertion:

> A group of companies and interested persons known informally as the Java Tourist and Development Survey have combined to investigate the feasibility of establishing a complex of industries at the

port of Tjilatjap in Indonesia… If the venture shall prove feasible the parties shall have a pre-emptive right to establish and carry on a tourist industry and ancillary businesses at the location including fishing and boating enterprises and other activities designed to enhance the prospects of a tourist resort.

Rollo was certainly a busy man at this stage of his career. But even a busy and resourceful man needs an income stream sufficient to cover his daily expenses. Rollo and his partner in the estate agency, Phil Trouchet, had little in the way of office staff and equipment but there is always rent and fuel and household expenses to be met. It was probably just as well that Rollo and Jill were now able to move into the family home at 2 Adams Road with Melissa and Jeremy so that their equity in the premises at 3 Dartmouth Avenue could be put to use. The arrangement was that when Paul and Alix came to Perth from time to time in the course of their official duties they would stay at the Parmelia Hotel in the city.

My parents made their first visit to Perth soon after our trip to Canberra for the swearing-in ceremony and related events. They were committed to visiting each of the Australian states in turn and, in doing so, they had resolved that in addition to the more formal occasions involving politicians and other leading citizens there should also be a pattern of informal get-togethers with younger people who were making a mark in the community. With that thought in mind, in early July, Paul and Alix hosted a buffet dinner at the Parmelia Hotel to which Rollo and I and our respective wives were invited. The guests were a cross-section of up-and-coming business people, well-known farmers, leading athletes, student leaders and representatives of the legal and medical professions. Many of these were known to us, as was the journalist, Pippa Johnson, who covered the event for the morning newspaper.

Pippa's account of the evening was accompanied by pictures reflecting the personalities and garments mentioned in her text.

Trouser suits and sputnik lighting set the tone of the young-set party at the Parmelia ballroom last night. Gay Cook, wife of Claremont footballer Lorne Cook, set the pace when she arrived in a flowing long black and white silk culotte. She was followed by Michael Ahern's pretty young wife Jo, wearing a richly coloured brocade trouser suit with a lilac shirt and dangling pendant. Dr Peter Nattrass's attractive blonde wife Margot said that she tossed up between wearing a black cutaway dress and a long white dress, then decided to play safe and wear the white, as a dress more suitable for the occasion.

The Pippa Johnson report went on to say,

Despite some of the trendy outfits worn by the more daring guests the fashion honours went to Jenny Edwards, wife of author-diver Hugh Edwards. Her body-hugging silver tunic dress worn over matching pants was a stunner. The Parmelia ballroom with its vivid orange and red tonings and sputnik lights provided a perfect setting for the glittering occasion. Informality was the keynote. Sir Paul sat at one table and Lady Hasluck at another and guests took it in turns to sit with them for one of the three courses. Many of the guests lingered until midnight.

In addition to the guests singled out for their striking attire, the guest list included other familiar names and with a short note as to what they had achieved: Mr and Mrs Tony Manford (Olympic yachting), Mr and Mrs Frank Baden-Powell (theatre), Mr and Mrs Kevin Merifield (football and business), Mr Rennie Lee-Steere (farming), Mr Terry Burke (Labor MLA), Mr and Mrs F. Chaney (solicitor, Liberal Party), Mr Stephen Errington (Young Country Party League), Mr Tim Knowles (journalist), Mr and Mrs Denis Marshall (football) Mr Philip May (Olympic athlete), Paul Monger (farming), Miss Susan Boyd (President Guild of Undergraduates), Mr Philip Gardiner (senior student St George's College) and senior students from the other university colleges.

It was a memorable night, but it was followed soon afterwards by a night of far greater significance. The goal voiced by President John F. Kennedy some years earlier – to put a man on the moon – was finally brought to fruition. For Rollo and others of my generation this was a never-to-be-forgotten moment in our lives.

Like countless others in Perth, no doubt, Sally and I turned on our TV set after dinner, not quite sure whether we in Western Australia would be receiving live coverage of the lunar module's landing, a critical moment for Neil Armstrong and Buzz Aldrin, although we knew from earlier events, including John Glenn's famous flight, that Australian tracking stations had an important part to play.

Coverage of the crucial events was expected to begin in our corner of the world at about two a.m. While waiting for the appointed hour, we sat watching an old black and white thriller starring the British actor George Sanders. It was followed by an equally incongruous tale: an American war movie featuring Edward G. Robinson dressed up as a naval officer, barking commands at ratings on the lower deck. By the time this finished, the appointed hour had passed.

I confess to dozing off while the periodic updates ran on. The next time I looked up, I suddenly realised that the surface of the moon was there in our room, a pitted grey surface hovering eerily in the eye of the camera with the vast black void beyond. A rounded section of the lunar module's porthole was on the screen also, a frame of sorts for the alien landscape, although the presence of the porthole added a powerful sense of authenticity to what we were being told: the eagle has landed.

We were given pictures of the control room at Houston, and some audio of the astronauts' voices, but didn't seem to be getting any pictures of the touchdown. When they came, they brought with them a nerve-racking sense of tension until it was clear that the landing had been safely accomplished. The cramped space within the module meant that it would be several hours before the astronauts could finalise their suiting-up process and be ready to emerge. It became clear to me that, by the time this happened, I would be at work.

But no matter. We were all of one mind at the office as to what we should do. A group of us, staff and clients alike, formed a semicircle around a TV set mounted on a table in the back room. Rollo had called in to drop off some documents and joined the group. We stood there, silently, awe-struck, mesmerised by the black and white images floating across the screen as the riveting events were presented to us – the desolate moonscape, the dark void beyond, the search for a boulder-free landing site, the nerve-racking seconds as the fuel ran out while the search for a site went on, the miracle of the landing itself, the eventual hazy image of a bulky figure clambering down to the moon's surface. Then, Neil Armstrong's famous first words: 'That's one small step for man; one giant leap for mankind.'

We watched the replays with fascination: the tentative footsteps of these builders in space, the imprints of their clumsy boots in the shallow dust, the positioning of a plaque by their tiny, airless flag: 'Here men from the planet earth first set foot on the moon. We came in peace for all mankind.' Though little was said as we in our group at the office listened to the ongoing commentary and stared at the screen, we probably sensed that this was a moment in time that might never be surpassed for those who were seeing it happen, as if we ourselves, like millions of others on earth, were participants in a transcendental awakening.

For a later generation, of course, the images are on the record, easily accessible if required. But they now seem quite different to what we saw that day, and the mood is certainly not the same. The images have become a matter of history. They have been fitted into the flow of momentous events and are viewed accordingly, with a degree of detachment.

One has to remember also that in the end most lives are affected more by what is happening nearby on a daily basis than by singular events that loom large for a moment, until, within a few weeks or months, they begin to seem unreal, or too far away to really matter. There is something of this in a poem my father wrote called 'Space Probe', in which he compares the unworldly experience of heroic astronauts with the situation of a watcher on earth, at ease on a hillside, enjoying a familiar scene.

> You went away loudly and have come back
> to the small hushed ripples of the sea.
> You have explored the surface of the moon
> and outer space and gazed on silvery earth
> from far away, found stars beyond the stars,

> and still know nothing more than I have known
> on one small hilltop, drowsing at midday
> where on a swaying thistle stalk
> a winter robin perched,
> and the brilliant declaration of its breast
> shone as a revelation of all life.
>
> The emptiness of space
> shrinks to the fullness of this patch.
> Here flames the red-breast truth.
> From here the living Me,
> lifted in exaltation,
> inhabits without vehicle the whole universe
> hearing the singing sound of space unlimited
> and the small noise of beetles in the grass.

Not surprisingly, then, at the end of our moon-watching morning, the TV set was taken off the table in the back room. Within a short time, everyone was going about their business in the usual way.

A month or so later I was held in thrall by a landing of an entirely different kind – I am speaking metaphorically – this time on earth. The arrival of my second son: Lindsay Robert Hasluck. While Sally lay in the Devonleigh Hospital at Cottesloe, Rollo treated me to a celebratory lunch.

A return of the astronauts, a splashdown in the sea, a new arrival on the home front, celebratory drinks. These were all welcome, but things kept moving on. The West Australian nickel boom, inspired by the run on Poseidon shares, was now well and truly under way. Rob Holmes à Court, my ingenious partner, was setting up companies for a wide range of developers, would-be miners and managerial consultants for one venture after another. At the other end of the office, I spent most of my time looking after Rollo's affairs and attending to the firm's court work. In my mind's eye, I can still see Rob at this stage of our joint venture, sitting at his desk in the front room – a former laboratory for industrial chemists – surrounded by developers and mining men, talking about their bright ideas, the discoveries to be made, the profits to be distributed, an inscrutable but faintly mischievous expression on his face. His loyal secretary, Val Pitman, was always on hand to bring him a fresh pack of cigarettes, more coffee.

I was never quite sure what Rob was up to, although I knew he was taking an intense interest in the stock market. He had virtually given up court work by now, while as I had my head down assembling evidence and proofing witnesses. Indeed, it was at this time, led by Peter Durack as senior counsel, that I became involved in a long-running battle to obtain a rehearing before a Court of Marine Inquiry on behalf of George Page, the master of a Rottnest Island ferry. The court case arose out of a collision on the Swan River between two ferries: the MV *Andrew* commanded by Page and the MV *Katameraire*. When a preliminary issue concerning the form of the rehearing was taken to the Full Court, we were opposed by the Solicitor General, Sir Ronald Wilson, who later became the first West Australian to be appointed to the High Court. The judgement of the Full Court in our favour was one of the few instances where the name M.R.H Holmes à Court & Co. appeared in the law reports.

When the matter was sent back to the Court of Marine Inquiry, Peter Durack and I drew upon Rollo's boating experience in presenting the case for George Page, but we probably needed more than good advice to win. In the end the Court of Marine Inquiry found that Page's ferry, the MV *Andrew*, left the Barrack Street jetty at Perth a few minutes before the MV *Katameraire* with both craft then engaging in a furious race to Fremantle, where the first to arrive would collect most of the passengers bound for Rottnest.

The *Katameraire* was gaining on the *Andrew* and turned at the inner Dolphin near Perth Yacht club to take a short cut to Armstrong Spit. To maintain her advantage, the master of the *Andrew* then set a course across the course of the *Katameraire* to force her to pass behind. There was a collision at a point short of the Armstrong Spit which forced the *Katameraire* off-course. Despite the danger to passengers, the master of the *Andrew* left the wheel unattended to argue with members of the *Katameraire* crew before putting the wheel back on a collision course. The master of the *Katameraire* then stopped his engines and gave way to the *Andrew*.

The court held that the *Andrew*, as a crossing ferry, was obliged to keep out of the way of the *Katameraire*. But the master of the *Katameraire* also had a duty to avoid a collision by reducing speed and passing behind when it became apparent to him that the *Andrew* was not obeying the crossing rule and was on a collision course. Both masters were to blame for the casualty, with the result that the charge of misconduct against George Page had been established.

Rollo was not the only one to help us in presenting the case. Rob Holmes à Court, always courteous, took an interest in the issues when we met for lunch occasionally. He was a clever man and had a gift for thinking outside the square, a way of looking at things with a fresh eye, so I was inclined to listen to his views attentively. He was skilled in the art of persuasion, although he had no wish to be an advocate, confined to a courtroom day after day. I was conscious also that in his usual mischievous way, the style of a contrarian, he saw the mad race to Fremantle in search of custom as a sign of the times, a signal to would-be winners in a brand-new era to take whatever risks were necessary. In our lunchtime discussions, we would begin by looking at the logic of the relevant rules, whether an overtaking vessel could also be a crossing vessel, but somehow, in the end, we always seemed to finish up talking about commercial takeovers and the money to be made accordingly.

Rob was fascinated by the activities of Slater and Walker, at that time the best-known corporate raiders in Great Britain, and he talked about them incessantly. Had I kept my wits about me, I would have detected that this was not just idle lunch hour chit-chat, this was where Rob's mind and energies were headed. I listened patiently, doing my best to keep an attentive expression fixed to my face.

The attentive expression was soon replaced by a look of horror. I opened the newspaper one morning to find that Rob had bought a controlling interest in Albany Woollen Mills for what in those days seemed to be a colossal price. I knew little about his financial resources but doubted that they would stretch to this. Oddly enough, on the day in question, Rob was away so it was left to me and some of my colleagues in the firm to fend off the media. There we were, in our little office opposite the bowling alley, suddenly besieged by journalists and camera men, but without knowing anything about the matter in hand.

A degree of order was restored the following day when Rob returned. But it was then revealed that Albany Woollen Mills was heavily indebted to the state government. The premier and his ministers were threatening to put in a receiver should Holmes à Court, the incoming purchaser, do an asset strip and threaten local jobs.

'What are you going to do about the debt?' we asked.

'I'll think of something,' Rob said, with a characteristically enigmatic grin.

Within a few days, chess-player style, he had charmed the premier, Sir Charles Court, and appeased the chairman of the company, Ernest Lee-Steere. Upping the ante, he had even borrowed funds to purchase new equipment, thus making the mills profitable eventually, a source of local employment. In the meantime, back at the office, the rest of us were prostrate with nervous exhaustion.

Shortly after this, M.R.H. Holmes à Court & Co. split up. It had become apparent to me and two of my colleagues in the firm that our senior partner, to all intents and purposes, would soon be abandoning the law for business. There were other factors at work too. I didn't think like Rob. I didn't have a nerve of steel. I didn't like buying things when I didn't know where the money was coming from. I wanted to go on practising law, but not while being besieged by the press. The business scene wasn't for me. We decided to go our separate ways.

I moved to a medium-sized law firm that soon became Keall Brinsden, a firm comprised mainly of friends and contemporaries from Law School. We got on well together and it was pleasing that a number of them were known to my brother Rollo from other days, so I was able to continue doing his conveyancing work as required.

In the meantime, of course, Rob Holmes à Court was steadily building his business empire, setting the scene for various takeovers and attempted takeovers that attracted nationwide attention and permitted him to amass a fortune. Bell Resources, Ansett Airlines, BHP, theatres in the West End of London, newspapers, racehorses, art collections – it all seemed to be going so well, until he too was drawn into the confusion known as WA INC and damaged by the global financial crash that dragged down so many of the other big-hitters. But I will pass over all of that, for it isn't part of my story. It belongs to a different book.

In this book, I am looking principally at my brother's life and times, the paths he took and the way he lived. Unfortunately, Rollo's situation in the early 1970s wasn't quite as bright as before. On various fronts, things weren't proceeding as smoothly as he might have wished.

The Next Phase

For many people in the Perth business world, 1970 began as a year rich with potential. Iron ore projects in the Pilbara were expanding and the Poseidon share price bonanza meant that nickel was a name to conjure with. The search for mineral sands in the south-west of the state was proceeding steadily as I discovered shortly after parting company with Holmes à Court. A first job with my new firm was to seek an injunction on behalf of Cable Sands NL against a Japanese dredging contractor whose work on harbour extensions at Bunbury was a threat to stockpiles of minerals sands awaiting export at the harbour's edge.

The real estate community was busy also. Some of Rollo's projects had been completed, but others had been hindered by delay in planning and finance approvals. New office blocks were under way in the city and nearby suburbs, which made it difficult for Rollo and his partners to find suitable tenants for their two comparatively small office developments in Rokeby Road, Subiaco. Delays led to certain syndicate members becoming restive, which meant that a good deal of time and energy had to be expended in placating worries and apprehensions.

Jill's modelling career was taking up more time than in earlier years and it led also to an audition at the local Channel 7 television station to work on air as a presenter of the weather news. She won the part and, in popular parlance, became a weather girl: a role that brought with it a new and different set of friends, and introductions to various celebrities. The change in her circumstances may have added to an existing mood of strain on the home front, although this was not enough, of itself, to dissuade Rollo from having a good time if there was a party to attend or if a boat trip to Rottnest with some of his friends could be managed. He loved being surrounded by a group of friends, male and female alike, keeping his audience amused with fishing tales, talk of ferry collisions, near misses, stories of any kind that would swell the store of communal recollections.

Not surprisingly, the store of recollections included tales about some of his own mishaps and near misses. One of these concerned an incident at Rottnest that might have struck less adventurous souls as a forewarning of even greater risks to come. But that wasn't Rollo's way of looking at things. It was just another story, the sort of thing that happened to anyone who was out there, testing the elements.

The daily paper provided a graphic account of the incident in question.

> Mr Rollo Hasluck. The son of the Governor-General, Sir Paul Hasluck narrowly escaped serious injury when gale force winds and a raging surf pounded his launch on to the beach at Rottnest. Witnesses said last night Mr Hasluck and two other men were sleeping aboard the 32ft launch which had been moored about 150 yards off shore in Thomson Bay. The boat's mooring snapped. It was picked up by the winds and seas and driven towards the beach.
>
> The boat clipped the end of the jetty as the seas carried it careering towards the beach. One witness said the boat came crashing through the waves like a surf boat. The surf picked up the launch near the beach and pounded it into the sand about five feet above the high water mark.
>
> Mr Hasluck and the other two men escaped with minor cuts and abrasions. Mr Ernie Shardlow who raised the alarm, said that the incident occurred at about 10 p.m. He said: 'It all happened so quickly they didn't have time to start the motors. I don't even know if they woke up.'
>
> Members of the Rottnest Island Board said last night the weather had prevented many holidaymakers going to the island. They said only 150 people arrived in yesterday's ferries. The weekend was one of the quietest three-day holidays at the island on record.

It was at about this time that Rollo and Jill decided to live separately for a while, although it was by no means clear to me or to other members of their respective families what lay behind the rift or how deep it was. Jill's parents had left York and were now living in Claremont, quite close to 2 Adams Road, as Dr Jim Munro was affected by a heart condition. Jill moved to their home in Bay Road with the two children and Rollo stayed where he was in the Hasluck family home.

Lorna Munro and my parents had done what they could to avert the separation, but to no avail. For Paul and Alix, of course, their distance from the troubled domestic scene hindered the playing of an effective role, as did the demands of their official duties. Coincidentally, towards the end of 1971, as if to underline their distance from the scene, they were invited to represent the Australian nation at a unique gathering of heads of state, the like of which may never be seen again: a celebration at the ancient site of Persepolis in Iran of the 2,500th anniversary of the Persian empire of Cyrus the Great, King of Kings.

They flew to the city of Shiraz and from there were driven to what looked like the setting of a massive mediaeval tournament: large yellow circular tents flying the flags of many nations in the vicinity of a central plaza occupied by a majestic banqueting tent. They were conducted to the saluting dais by the Shah of Iran, where Paul took the salute and the national anthems of Australia and Iran were played. While waiting in the wings, Alix was told by the empress that the royal couple had been performing these ceremonial receptions throughout the entire day for one after another of the arriving celebrities and it was very tiring.

Cars were laid on next morning to take the official visitors to Persepolis, the ruins of the palace of Cyrus, consisting of an enormous stone terrace with carvings showing row upon row of soldiers, bowmen and spearmen with occasional chariots and camels. Paul and Alix went on from there to see the tomb of Xerxes high on a rock face some distance away. The state dinner took place that night in the splendid banqueting tent with the catering done by Maxims of Paris. A speech was made by the Shah, to which the Emperor Haile Selassie of Ethiopia responded, as the most senior of the heads of state in attendance.

The next phase of the celebrations was the grand military parade, which was held at the ruins a day later, with the guests being assigned to rows of seats arranged below the great stone terrace. The Shah told the gathering that Iran remained true to its mission to carry the message of Cyrus's tolerance and understanding to the world. As his amplified voice faded away into the mountains behind the columns of the ancient palace, drums began to beat, and music, dissonant and awe-inspiring, came from a group of musicians robed and bearing huge trumpets of a peculiar, archaic shape. The parade was led by standard bearers in gold-edged red robes from the earliest period of Persian history and was made up of the soldiers and chariots of dynasty after dynasty advancing in perfect formation.

On the following day, all the guests left for Teheran in special aircraft, some to continue their voyage home, others to stay for the inauguration of the Shayad monument by the Shah and the opening of a giant sports stadium on the outskirts of the capitol.

The poet Shelley, in a well-known poem about the transience of imperial fame, points to an inscription on a ruined statue of Ozymandias, King of Kings, who was thought to possess incomparable power: 'Look on my works ye mighty and despair.' But the poem concludes, 'Nothing beside it remains. The lone and level sands stretch far away.'

It is an inevitable characteristic of history, Shelley's poem suggests, that monuments and supposedly permanent regimes rise and fall, leaving behind only vestiges of what they once were. It is a well-known fact of history that within a few years of the celebrations at Persepolis the Shah of Iran was overthrown, a fate which also befell Haile Selassie in Ethiopia. But the notion of continuity, the importance of keeping things together, if possible, by marking special occasions or remembering the good times and former achievements, is deeply embedded in the minds of most people.

Something of this may have played a part in the renewed attempts made by my parents upon their return from overseas, and of Lorna Munro also, to mend fences and find some means of repairing the relationship between Rollo and Jill. One way or another, arrangements were made for the children of the marriage, Melissa and Jeremy, to live with my parents at Government House and for Melissa to go to school in Canberra. This would allow for Rollo and Jill to spend six months or so travelling together in England and Europe. If all went well, the prospect was that they would patch up their differences and, upon returning to Perth, resume their married life. These arrangements were quickly put in place and, after a short stopover in Singapore, they arrived at Gatwick airport on 30 January 1972.

Travels are always exciting, the travellers' senses fully alert, minds and bodies ready for action. One never knows what to expect – as it was when Rollo and I set forth to cross the Nullarbor – but one hopes for the best. For Rollo and Jill, on this occasion, it would be a matter for them as to whether they would have enough time and energy left at the end of each day to address the underlying purpose of the trip, and to work out what had to be done about their relationship. Or would they be overwhelmed by it all? Enthralled by ancient sites and obscure inscriptions? It was up to them.

They began by renting a flat in Kangaroo Valley at 130 Earl's Court Road, West Kensington. According to Rollo, in his first letter home, they found the Underground system easy to manage and quickly started visiting some of the usual tourist attractions: Tower of London, Buckingham Palace, Westminster Abbey, Royal Mews, London Silver Vaults. They spent what Rollo called an amusing afternoon at Speakers' Corner in Hyde Park but were less impressed with that other forum for oratory, the Houses of Parliament – too many tourists.

In the first fortnight, they were kept busy in the evenings by attending a variety of plays in the West End: *Oh! Calcutta*, *Getting On* starring Kenneth More, Agatha Christie's long-running play *The Mousetrap*, John Mortimer's *A Voyage Around My Father* featuring Alec Guinness, *The Threepenny Opera* with Vanessa Redgrave and *Sleuth* with Marcus Goring. Rollo's personal key to ratings awarded the worst score to *The Mousetrap*.

Their flat in Earl's Court Road soon proved unsatisfactory, so they looked around for something else. Their friends from Perth, Peter and

Margot Nattrass, helped out by offering some temporary accommodation in their flat at 89 Drayton Gardens in Chelsea. At that time Peter, having qualified as a doctor in Australia, was completing some further medical studies in London. His wife Margot was working in the fashion department at Harrods during the day but was principally committed to cordon bleu classes in the evening. Peter and Margot's hospitality ran on for a while and in the end became virtually a home base for Rollo and Jill as they did some travelling.

First up, they arranged to visit their friend from Canberra days, Philip Wheeler, who was now at Brasenose College, Oxford, studying Classics. He and his wife Donelle showed Rollo and Jill the sights, which included a tour of Wadham College, where I was enrolled in the mid-sixties. I still have on my mantelpiece a photo of Rollo standing at the entrance to Wadham College in a pale, padded jacket, the huge wooden portals of the college looming behind him. They drove on to the nearby town of Woodstock for a visit to Blenheim Palace.

Rollo provided further details in a letter home.

> The next day Philip and Nell had to go to work so they lent us their car for the day. We drove down to Winchester and saw the cathedral (fabulous old building). Then Jill and I went to an old 11th century church called St Cross and did two 13th century brass rubbings. It took hours but they look quite good. We're going to do lots more as we travel and bring them home to sell for $20 each. From Winchester we drove to Salisbury and then to Stonehenge (what a phizzhog!!!). I guess I'd expected something bigger and more impressive. From there back to Oxford.
>
> Took the train back to London. On Wednesday we picked up our Motor Caravan – Austin J2 Hadrian 30cwt. Contains double bed, table, sink, stove, toilet and loads of cupboard space. We collected the van from Brixton and got hopelessly lost trying to get back to Kensington. This weekend we are going for a trial run to Cambridge and back. If it performs okay we'll head for Scotland. Writer's cramp is attacking me – ahhh!! Give a big hug and kiss to Melissa and Jer from both of us and tell them that we think of them constantly. Love from us both. Rollo.

Jill wrote to my parents on the same day.

> Will only write a short note as Rollo has done a marvellous job – he has spent the past half hour admiring his work: the first letter he had written in years… We are going out with Margot and Peter Nattrass tonight and they are also taking us to Portobello Road… We were having a few drinks at a small place called Julie's Place and Pippa Johnson, a journalist friend of Rollo's walked in. Great excitement as we had been trying to contact her for weeks. Almost the same as being back in Perth again. We are seeing so many people. We rang Sue Harkness this evening as she is off to Ireland for a week, then off to Vienna… Hope the children are being good and we are glad to hear that they are well and happy.

The van worked well, but their plans changed. Instead of going to Scotland, they went to Wales for a few days, where they visited centres such as St Davids, Pembroke and Swansea. According to Rollo, they spent an interesting night at Aberystwyth.

> The town caravan park was closed but the proprietor's son suggested a nice spot down by the beach near the mouth of the river. We drove down there about 6 p.m. and found a nice spot with the river on one side and the ocean on the other. About 10 p.m. we were playing cards when we were conscious of a noise like running water. I opened the van door and just about stepped into the river which had risen about thirty feet in a few hours, and on the other side the ocean wasn't much further away. We started the engine and drove to high ground safely. The tidal differences are quite colossal. In the morning we could see the area where we had been parked was completely under water.

It seems that it rained so much in Wales that they both got the flu and ended up in bed on doctor's orders, staying with the Wheelers in Oxford. It is pleasing to know that for once in his life Rollo was prepared to obey doctor's orders, but this interlude didn't hold them back. They set off for Paris and, apart from their caravan dropping an exhaust pipe on the motorway to Dover, it wasn't long before they had crossed the channel by ferry and found a place for their van at a caravan park in the Bois de

Boulogne. This set the scene for five days of Parisan sightseeing, including a visit to the Australian Ambassador to France, Alan Renouf, who had been with my father in New York in the 1940s and had known Rollo as a boy.

From Paris, they drove through the Loire Valley, then further south to where the Spanish border meets the Mediterranean Sea. They crossed the border to begin a six-day stay at a camp on the outskirts of Barcelona. Their sightseeing included a visit to a bullfighting arena where, to Rollo, the contest seemed one-sided. 'By the time the sixth bull came on I was hoping he would win. He gored the matador and stomped on him. The crowd cheered.'

They moved north to the Costa Brava and chanced upon a charming little village called Tossa del Mar with a fabulous beach, an old castle guarding the bay and some tasty paella prepared from sea food they saw coming straight off the fishing boats that beached about nine o'clock each morning.

Then back to France.

> We reached Marseilles at nightfall. It was a beautiful sight driving down the mountain, looking across the city and the harbour lights. We camped for the night on the side of a rugged mountain, perched like a couple of buzzards waiting for the city to die so that we could pounce on it. It died the very next morning when it looked drab and like any other large city.

They moved on to Hyeres on the south coast of France. Before leaving England they had met some Aussie blokes who had entered their Soling (an Olympic-class yacht) in a regatta to be held at Hyeres in early April, so Rollo and Jill were keen to see them again and share some of the excitement before going on to Monte Carlo and Italy. Rollo ended a long letter to his parents from Hyeres with a note to this effect:

> As I write this, looking out the window about twenty yards away, are two little girls about Melissa's age picking flowers of which there are an abundance in this camp. It's times like this when we would love to have the children with us, and they would really enjoy it

too. After Rome we hope to go across to Greece depending on our finances. Here's Jill with a few more words: Dear Paul and Alix – just a note tacked on to Rollo's marvellous effort – not much left for me to say again. Lots of children around. Give our love to them.

Upon reaching Rome, they got in touch with Geoffrey Pretyman, the protocol officer who had been with my parents in their early days at Government House but was now back in the diplomatic service. According to Rollo, he saw them off with 'a bottle of Scotch and a carton of fags' as they drove on to Naples, then to Sorrento, a visit enhanced by an enjoyable day on the offshore Isle of Capri.

They crossed the Adriatic Sea by ferry on their way to Dubrovnik, that picturesque walled city situated on a promontory on the west coast of what was then the communist regime of Yugoslavia. They had by now abandoned any thought of going on to Greece. Rollo described their arrival in Dubrovnik and related events in this way:

> The customs and passport inspection was the most rigorous we had experienced and took about twenty minutes as a guy pulled everything in our van to pieces. Even pulled seat covers off and looked under the chassis.
>
> It was a clear blue sky and the water looked fabulous although the temperature was only about 65 degrees Farenheit. During this time we went to inspect a 14th century fortress overlooking the small old city port. When we arrived at the fortress we found a school class in musical appreciation being conducted in the main hall – we were allowed entrance when we explained that we were visitors from Australia – and for the next hour were entertained by a thirty piece orchestra playing Yugoslavian instruments. It really was most enjoyable. I think most of the students found us an enjoyable distraction also. We spent the night at Dubrovnik in the van and next day took a ride around the city in a small boat we hired. We found everything surprisingly cheap and managed to stock up on food supplies quite cheaply.
>
> A day later we left Dubrovnik and headed north along the coast by a very picturesque but rather hazardous road and spent the next night at a city called Split in a very good camping area – one of the

few in Yugoslavia. It was at this point that we found out about the smallpox epidemic in the north of Yugoslavia. All travellers were being stopped by police and with health cards being examined. We hadn't seen a newspaper since Rome and knew nothing of it. Anyway we were warned to stay on the coast road and get out of the country as soon as possible. We put in a long day driving and reached Rijeka for the night, camping by the roadside. Next morning we zoomed into Italy through Trieste and on to Venice.

They spent several days in Venice, stopped off at Florence, went north to Innsbruck in Austria, and on to Munich in Germany, where preparations were under way for the Olympic Games. They crossed the Rhine at Karlsruhe, drove to Luxembourg, and cut across the top of France to board the ferry. On reaching London, 'we crashed in on Peter and Margot Nattrass and had our first hot shower for over two weeks'.

While writing home, Rollo had touched on what might happen eventually on the domestic front. In his usual enthusiastic and perhaps overly optimistic way he had even canvassed the possibility of arrangements being made for Melissa and Jeremy to join them on some further travels, including a trip to Africa. To this, my father penned what was obviously a very carefully considered reply.

> As I have said on previous occasions, I cannot have any right to intervene in matters between you and Jill, although I would try to be as helpful as you might wish me to be at any time. In respect of the grandchildren I have a different claim to have a concern with their welfare. From what I have seen of them daily in the past two months, and the little I saw of them in the preceding months in Perth, they are both badly in need of stability and normalcy in their lives.
>
> If it were not for the children, I would say that your lives are your own and that you could plan with regard only to your own interests. But because of the children your lives are not your own. You have to plan for them too. An understanding was that you and Jill would be back in Australia by the end of June and that, having worked out your own relationship, you would be ready to set up home again and to have the children with you… Both your mother

and I are strongly against the idea you mentioned in your letter of bringing the children to London with us and letting them travel with you for the next six months or so, returning to Perth at the end of the year from South Africa... The idea of dragging them along with you in a journey through Africa, including countries that are practically unsettled, just appals us.

Even if the practical difficulties did not exist my view is that the interruption of the normal way of life would be very disturbing for the children and would have bad emotional effects on them. They are deeply in need of stability... You have many years ahead of you and probably later you will be able to travel again, either with them or after putting them in boarding school, without harm to them and with more joy for yourselves... It may be fun to keep on travelling but you have to weigh that fun against other demands.

One of the chief arguments in favour of your trip overseas was that it would help you to work out your relationship. I think you ought to tell us frankly if the hope for a full reconciliation of your marriage is going to be realised. If you do not have that starting point when you come back then most of what I have said falls down. All that I have written is written with deep affection and with continued loyalty to you as a son.

It seems that this letter brought to an end any further talk of travels in Africa. Rollo and Jill loved their children, so Paul's wise counsel carried the day. It was probably foreseen on both sides that when Paul and Alix were on leave in London mid-year there would be further exchanges, face to face, about what the future held. In the meantime, however, while at the Nattrass flat in Chelsea, Rollo was setting out in a letter home some more immediate plans.

Our plans are to stay in London till 10th May, or 14th at the latest. During this time I will sell the van (after I've fixed it up) and we'll buy as smaller, faster station wagon (just big enough to sleep in the back of it). We then intend to head off to Europe again to drive straight to Spain – see Madrid and Grenada and the south coast, by ferry across to Morocco and back to Spain, drive up the other side through Portugal and back to England. We would see you briefly in London, early July, before we fly home.

They bought a small green Hillman Husky (6cwt, 875cc with room for two in the back) and went ahead as planned. While in Madrid, they stayed at the Australian embassy, as the ambassador, Dudley McCarthy, was an old friend of my father from the Department of External Affairs. They spent several weeks in Morocco which included a trip to the Algerian border. They couldn't cross the border but the documentation of their trip included a photo of Jill leaning against the shoulder of one of the border sentries in a nonchalant pose. It wasn't long before they were back in England.

Before leaving for Spain and Morocco, they had driven to the Cotswolds to stay with my parents-in-law, Robert and Irene Bolton, who lived in the small hamlet of Crimscote near Stratford-upon-Avon, surrounded by farming properties and lush green fields. They enjoyed the visit, according to Jill, and got on well with the Boltons, although Rollo was not entirely diplomatic at one stage when he declined an invitation to be taken around the various Shakespearean sites in the neighbourhood on the grounds that he wasn't particularly interested in that sort of thing: an odd response from a man who had been part of the theatre world in Perth, if only briefly. Perhaps he had been put off the Bard by the weird rendition of Hamlet in Tom Stoppard's play *Rosencrantz and Guildenstern Are Dead*, the play we saw in Sydney after visiting Admiralty House.

In any event, their link to the Bolton household meant that after Spain and Morocco they were able to leave the Hillman van with the Boltons. Some months later, by which time Sally and I were in England, we bought the van and used it for some European travels of our own.

Before they left London, Rollo and Jill were minded to repay Peter and Margot Nattrass for their hospitality over several months. As Rollo's parents had now arrived in England, arrangements were made to take the Nattrasses to dinner at the Savoy Hotel. This proved to be an unusual evening.

After a pre-dinner drink, the group descended to a table in the main dining room. The younger members of the group were surprised to find Princess Margaret sitting at a table nearby, and because my father was known to her, equally surprised to find their presence acknowledged with a fleeting royal nod. Lord Carrington, well-known to my father as the former British High Commissioner in Canberra, came across from another table to have a chat.

Jill often told the story in later life that at this stage, when it seemed that Paul and Alix knew everyone in the room, she happened to notice an elderly gentleman sitting by himself at a table nearby. He looked lonely, almost forlorn. She wondered aloud whether he should be invited to join the group at the Hasluck table as an act of goodwill.

'I don't think so,' my father explained. 'That's John Paul Getty, one of the richest men in the world. He often dines here, and everyone knows that he likes to dine alone.'

The telling of this story usually prompted Rollo, with his customary zest, to tell another story about John Paul Getty at the Savoy – a story said to be based on an actual incident, but probably apocryphal – which went like this.

A pushy young Australian businessman is at the Savoy on the brink of closing an important deal with some British tycoons, but he knows he needs something extra to get across the line. Noticing John Paul Getty at a table nearby, the Aussie has a flash of inspiration. So he excuses himself from his own table and approaches the American billionaire, very respectfully, to make an unusual request. 'You were young once yourself, sir, and you know what it takes to get started. When you leave your table would you be willing to place a hand on my shoulder as you pass by and say a friendly word. A small favour like that, treating me as a familiar figure in the world of big business, will be all I need.'

The old man, having listened attentively to all of this, and recalling his own early days, no doubt, the tough times back then, nods sympathetically. He agrees to act as requested. Elated, the youngster returns to his own table and keeps the negotiations going.

Sure enough, within a short time Getty folds his napkin and rises to leave. He places his aged hand on the shoulder of the youngster and says, 'Good to see you.'

To which, in a tone implying an even closer connection than previously agreed, the brash but ever-resourceful youngster ups the ante with a breezy reply, 'Piss off, Getty. Can't you see I'm trying to close a deal?'

Rollo liked to tell that story, and when he told it he always raised a laugh from those around him. Upon returning to Perth, however, he soon found that he himself was in need of assistance in completing various business projects and tying up loose ends. I am not sure what exactly Rollo and Jill said to my parents in London about the future of their relationship. The letters they wrote in the course of their travels certainly suggested that they got on well together throughout their sightseeing tour and thoroughly enjoyed the experience. For my part, after returning from our own travels, I was mainly concerned with helping Rollo to find a way through his increasingly tangled commercial affairs.

Ending

While Rollo was overseas, his business affairs had languished. The management of his estate agency had been taken over by a colleague in the firm, Rick Lisle, which brought with it a need to attend to the affairs of the various syndicates and Rollo's involvement in a number of related companies: Hasluck Investments Pty Ltd, Hasluck and Morrison Projects Pty Ltd and Palos Verdes Estates Pty Ltd. With some assistance from me while Rollo was away, Rick had toiled heroically to fend off bank managers and creditors and to fill vacancies in the two office blocks Yanderra House and Bindarra House.

Back in Perth, Rollo came reluctantly to the conclusion that his income stream had slowed to a trickle and it was all too much. He would have to look for other opportunities. While battling to enhance the prospects of his various projects, he applied for the position of contracts administrator with a local transport company. His submission contained a summary of his working life since leaving school and noted that 'during my past ten working years I have always held a position of responsibility and have had to work without supervision on my own initiative'.

This was one of several applications submitted to prospective employers at that time, but mostly to no avail. His perseverance was rewarded eventually by a letter from the state manager of the prominent real estate agency L.J. Hooker.

> We have pleasure in confirming your appointment to our Industrial, Commercial and Leasing department as from Monday next, 18 September 1972. Your remuneration will be as follows – salary $4000 per annum, car allowance $1000 per annum, commission rate 10% of office commission on all sales made by you.

This promised some respite from the financial difficulties he was grappling with, but didn't solve all his problems. By a letter dated 7 February 1973 he felt obliged to address a frantic plea to his mother:

> I'm writing to you because I've reached the stage where there is no one else to turn to. I am in extreme financial difficulty which was caused by a number of things about a year or so ago from which I haven't yet recovered and can see no way of doing so. I've reached the stage where very soon everything will close in on me so that I'll either end up in the Debtors Court or have to go into voluntary bankruptcy. Either way I'll probably lose my job over it, which I don't want to do because I like my job very much and I think I have a good future here.
>
> My present salary is more than adequate to live on and the prospects of it increasing in years to come are very good, but in the meantime I can't clear my debts. Unfortunately I am the victim of rather bad financial planning by myself some years ago when my business was buoyant i.e., all my assets are tied up in shares in companies and ventures which I can't get at or sell.

Fortunately for Rollo at this moment in time, Alix was in a position to provide her son with enough financial support to keep him afloat for the time being. She had recently inherited some shares from her maiden aunt in Queensland, Clarice Darker, the elderly aunt who had stayed with us in Perth ten years ago during the Empire Games. Alix's generous mood was probably enhanced by the fact that she had just brought out a book called *Royal Engineer* based on the life of Edmund DuCane, who had served as an engineer and magistrate in the early days of the Swan River colony. Her mood may even have been affected by the presence in her life of a basset hound called Gilmore, who she had acquired to accompany her on walks around the grounds of Government House. Gilmore's exploits were becoming well-known to us, including an occasion when the friendly basset disrupted a foreign ambassador's inspection of a guard of honour lined up on the front lawn of Government House by snuffing and drooling over the polished boots of the poker-faced guards until hastily removed from the scene by an aide-de-camp.

A shortage of funds was not the only issue on Rollo's agenda. The trip overseas had brought about a reconciliation of sorts in his domestic situation, true, but his financial anxieties meant that he wasn't well-placed to secure the relationship with his wife. Whatever the reason, Rollo and Jill went back to their old ways, their different circles of friendship. Rollo had sold his launch *Aristotle II* to raise some cash and was now at the wheel of a smaller but faster vessel, *Red Baron*, a move that was generally approved by the boating crowd. Jill had her friends from the television world. They had drifted apart and were living separately again. The children were back in Perth, attending Dalkeith Primary School, cared for by both parents, but living with Jill. The future of the marriage seemed uncertain.

There was talk of divorce. I knew next to nothing about matrimonial proceedings and, in any event, being too close to it all, would not have been inclined to advise or counsel either party. Rollo went to see David Anderson, my former principal at Lohrmann, Tindal and Guthrie for some preliminary advice. It takes a very experienced legal practitioner to gain even a faint understanding of the complexities of married life and of the very private factors bearing upon the erosion of a relationship. The factors in this case were particularly difficult to decipher. I came to no conclusion about them at that time, and have never done so. One was simply left with pragmatic questions of the kind an experienced practitioner is accustomed to deal with. What is to be done? What is the best way to keep things on an even keel, for the parties, for the children, and for the future?

Towards the end of March 1973, in a carefree moment, Sally and I decided to hold a party at our home enlivened by an eccentric title: At Last…the 78 rpm Show! The invitation we sent out to our friends, which was covered with facsimiles of old time record labels, made it clear that 'Admission is by tender of one used 78 rpm disc of dubious quality from any decade other than the present. The management reserves a right of veto in respect of madrigals and ukulele ensembles.'

Our guests arrived with a weird array of black shellac discs under their arms, retrieved from dark recesses and remote cupboards, no doubt, protected mostly by old brown paper wraps or faded record covers, bearing, as we had hoped, a range of unusual titles from the 1930s or a little later. 'My Blue Heaven', 'Boogie Woogie Birmingham Boy', 'My Canary Has Circles Under Its Eyes'… And the prize exhibit (by acclamation): 'I Wanna Dance Wif the Man Wot Brung Me'.

Rollo was there, bright-eyed and bushy-tailed as usual, all set for a good time. The joint collection of 78 rpm discs from our youth at 2 Adams Road had long since been vested in me because, of the two of us, I was the one who still had a record player capable of playing not only 33 rpm LPs (long-playing records) and 45 rpm 'doughnuts' but also the now generally obsolete 78 rpm discs. To cover the prescribed tender price for admission, I had, for old times' sake, handed back to Rollo the first record he had ever bought: 'When the Saints Go Marching In' by the Graham Bell Australian jazz band.

It was a fun party and ran on quite late. While standing with Rollo on the front veranda, beers in hand, he told me he was planning to take a short break, head off for a while, slip up to Singapore with some friends from school days at Scotch, Tim Knowles and Peter Halliday, and another friend, Don Roper. They would join one of the so-called 'Swingaway Tours' which were being advertised at a special price.

He went ahead with his plan although, even up to the day before departure, he was still trying to tie up some loose ends. Indeed, on the afternoon of that day, I went with him to the offices of Lohrmann, Tindal and Guthrie where he was to see David Anderson about his matrimonial situation. What a legal adviser says to his client is confidential, so I don't know what exactly took place between them. I thumbed through a magazine in the outer office and waited for Rollo to emerge. But I have in my own files a diary note about our visit which reads as follows: 'Rollo and Jill are no longer living together. Divorce proceedings have been initiated by Rollo but called off at the eleventh hour as it seems there is some possibility of a reconciliation.'

Rollo must have acquainted me with this summation as we left

David's office and went downstairs to St Georges Terrace. We stood there on the pavement near the old Perth Boys' School, opposite King Street, for a quick chat. He was leaving for Singapore early the next day and there were a few matters for me to attend to while he was away. His meeting with David seemed to have gone well and he was in good spirits, looking forward to his holiday. But he was coping with a heavy cold, flu perhaps, coughing occasionally. He hoped this wouldn't interfere with the plans he and his friends had in mind.

I wished him well as he turned away, not knowing that this was the last time I would see him. A message reached me a day or so later that they had got to Singapore safely and I thought no more about it. He had been to Singapore before and had travelled overseas. Why should I worry? I would see him back in Perth in due course.

I will turn now to the diary entry I made for Tuesday 5 June 1973.

> I get home from the office feeling whacked and resolve to have an early night. We are in bed reading, then a phone call. It is Dad. He has bad news. A message has just come from Singapore that Rollo has died suddenly. Collapsed and died. Like that. The details are scant but it seems he went to a doctor for his flu. Later, in the bar of his hotel, he complained of feeling unwell and collapsed. Dad rings off. It is raining outside and it rains all night. I weep for hours. I get up at dawn for a sip of water and look across the park to the faint light in the centre. He was meant to go for just a little while, but now he will never come back. Not ever. And this at a time when maybe he was on the brink of a fresh start.

A sudden death brings with it pandemonium. The radio had a newsflash about the tragedy. Phone calls started coming in, including an offer of assistance from Peter Mews, a son of the boat-building family by Claremont Jetty, now living in Singapore. It was some comfort to know that Rollo had been with close friends in Singapore. Dad rang again from Admiralty House in Sydney with some further details. These squared with a report that appeared in the newspaper, based on details provided by one of Rollo's travelling companions.

Mr Rollo Hasluck visited a Singapore doctor in the afternoon before his death on Tuesday night, according to *Daily News* journalist Tim Knowles who telephoned from Singapore today.

Mr Knowles said that Mr Hasluck was feeling too ill on Tuesday to join him and two other friends on a bus tour that included lunch. 'While we were out he went to a doctor and got some tablets,' said Mr Knowles. Later he went down to the bar and was having a drink with three Australian nurses when he collapsed.

A preliminary autopsy has revealed that Mr Hasluck died from heart failure. Mr Knowles said Mr Hasluck was suffering from influenza before the party left Perth. He was still feeling ill on Tuesday morning and went up to his hotel room telling his friends to leave without him if he did not come down to join the bus tour.

Mr Knowles, one of Mr Hasluck's closest friends, said the news of heart failure was a shock because he was a robust person, a strong swimmer and keen skin-diver. In Canberra today, Sir Paul Hasluck said he had been deeply touched by the many sympathy messages they had received from all parts of Australia.

In the days that followed, while condolence messages were still coming in, my father received a letter from Arthur Daley, an auctioneer in Inverell, New South Wales. He said,

> I wish to express my deepest sympathy on the death of your son. On that evening I was in the bar of the Ming Court Hotel when your son collapsed. I also gave heart massage with the assistance of three ladies who announced themselves as nurses from Melbourne while another man, unknown to me, gave him mouth to mouth resuscitation. I can assure you everything was done in our power to save your son. The biggest difficulty was trying to obtain a doctor and ambulance but they assured us at that at that hour the traffic was so heavy it was impossible to arrive at the hotel any earlier.

The Australian High Commission provided a full report a few days later, drawing upon the results of the autopsy and consultation with the nurses and a local pathologist, Dr Seah. It seems that Rollo had gone down to the bar where he encountered the nurses. 'He jokingly described the difficulties he had in communicating with the doctor.' He was prescribed Penbritin tablets and told the nurses that he understood these to be some sort of antibiotic. As they chatted, suddenly Rollo coughed, and appeared to be in some distress. 'He made a remark to the effect "Oh! That was a bit too deep!" He then collapsed, striking the bridge of his nose on some hard object as he fell.' Attempts were made to revive him. An ambulance arrived after he collapsed, but it was too late.

The report said that Rollo had died of acute myocarditis.

The pathologist, Dr Seah, explained that this condition is an inflammation of the muscles of the heart, which in this case probably resulted from some form of virus infection. The term acute denotes that the condition was not long standing. In all other respects Rollo appeared to very fit, and there appeared to be no connection between his heart attack and his having taken the Penbritin tablets.

A full account of this kind was worth having, because one never wishes to be haunted by doubts or suspicions. For myself, soon after the initial news came in, I couldn't help wondering whether what took place was affected to some extent by his personality, his habit of trying to get as much out of each day as he could possibly manage, his way of living. His friends went off, he stayed behind. After a short rest, feeling a little better perhaps, determined to enjoy every moment of his holiday, he went down to the hotel for a drink and began chatting to some nurses, the sort of thing he had done many times before. But this, of course, was mere speculation, and on that first day, in a state of confusion, I had to push aside such thoughts. There was a flow of incoming calls and the daily round doesn't stop.

I see from my diary that I drove my son Anthony to school and felt obliged to attend to some unavoidably urgent business at the office. By now the radio newsflash had been updated to include an excerpt from proceedings in the federal parliament in which Lionel Murphy, the Attorney General in the Whitlam government, called upon all Senators to join in a message of sympathy to the Governor-General. By lunchtime, the newspaper placard in the street bore the headline 'Tragic Death of Rollo Hasluck'. His boss, the manager of L.J. Hooker, rang me to express his sorrow and to say, quietly and very sincerely, that Rollo was a respected member of their staff. My father rang again with some information about transfer of the body to Perth and the funeral arrangements to be made.

I spent the evening writing a letter to my mother with some photos I thought she might like to have. Diary entries were a way of keeping busy, keeping grief at bay, so I said this about the letter I had just written.

> I include a photo of Rollo taken when we crossed the Nullarbor in 1960. He was very good looking then, slim and purposeful, holding up the bonnet of the Peugeot. A moment later he took a comedy shot of me pulling a long face and ostensibly lifting the car off my foot. What a trip it was. Coming out of Adelaide on the first day, heading for Port Pirie towards evening, we followed a station wagon. There were two bright-eyed, giggling girls in the back, snuggling under a tartan rug, peeping over the tailboard at the glare of our headlights. Rollo flicked our beam up and down a couple of times to make them dive for cover, still giggling. Weeping, I remember this. To forget one's brother would be to forget one's self. The tears come to my eyes all night.

Over the next few days, while arrangements for the funeral were being made, I began looking at what had to be done to sort out Rollo's affairs. I sat down with Rick Lisle and David Morrison and some of his other business associates. To my surprise, I found a multicoloured beach buggy parked in the garage at 2 Adams Road like some bright, oversized beetle, with a hire purchase agreement in the glovebox, but no clue as to why it was there or the use Rollo had in mind for it. Fishing from beaches, probably. Or perhaps it was simply another version of the ten-pound Chevrolet he had once acquired in a whimsical moment.

This and a few other discoveries made me realise, sadly, that I hadn't seen much of him since he and Jill had split up, except at my office in the city when he needed advice or there were documents to be signed. The house at 2 Adams Road was locked up and empty. The truth was that I didn't even know where he had been living of late.

It turned out that he had been sharing a flat with his friend Peter Halliday in Hawkstone Avenue, near the beach at North Cottesloe. Peter, who had been with him on the Swingaway tour, was back from Singapore by now and had begun packing up Rollo's clothes and other belongings. I called at the flat to see Peter and to make arrangements to have the various suitcases and boxes transferred to the playroom at 2 Adams Road, once the setting for get-togethers at a jaunty, make-believe varnished bar called Chez Rollo. The bar was still there but it hadn't been used for years. It wouldn't be used again. I found it very sad to be standing there with Peter as we surveyed the line of boxes and business suits on wire hangers, with Rottnest out there on the blue horizon.

I discovered also, to my even greater surprise, that a month or so before leaving for Singapore, Rollo had taken out a life insurance policy. He had surrendered his previous policies a few years ago, but here was a new one. The indications were, from what I knew of his affairs and what I was now finding out as I went along, that after discharging various liabilities, the estate would be left with few assets to pass on, but the proceeds of the policy were immune from the claims of his creditors. He was still married to Jill and she was the main beneficiary. It pleased me to know that he had made some provision for his wife and children.

I confess to often having wondered what prompted him to take out this policy, for prudent planning of this kind wasn't the sort of thing he usually got round to fixing up. It seemed to mirror the moment when, almost by chance, I took out a policy to cover the risk of injury to our children's carer, Sue Harkness. Or did he feel deep down ('That was a bit too deep,' he said) that something was amiss. The winding up of an estate usually brings with it a number of mysteries.

My parents were back from Admiralty House in Sydney and the day for the funeral had finally arrived. When a person dies young there is bound to be a huge turn out and this was the case on Monday 11 June 1973. Family members and his friends from all walks of life made the effort to attend, and for this we were grateful. I will turn to my diary for a full account of the day's events.

After lunch, a car from the funeral director's fleet comes to collect us: Jill, Sally and myself. A large black limousine with a noiseless quality to its engine and to everything about it. The passing traffic slides by silently as we drive on. We reach the premises of Bowra & O'Dea at the same time as my parents, conveyed to the funeral parlour by another car. While we inspect the various wreaths that have been delivered PH talks briefly to a federal parliamentarian who is representing the Prime Minister. After a while the sombre cars gather us up and we drive on through the back streets of Perth, towards the cemetery at Karrakatta.

Along the way, bystanders look on, uncomprehendingly. I stare back, feeling numb, affected by thoughts that lie too deep for tears. Love for a brother is a special kind of love. One depends on parents, but you grow up and, to some extent, you draw away from them. Love for a woman is active and requires nourishment. It is nurtured and replenished by reciprocity, give and take. But the love one has for a brother is undemanding. It is almost passive and, for that reason, it seems entirely dependable. It can be put to one side for a time and taken up again later, without effort. It comes from a shared experience and an outlook formed in the same era. It is different from other kinds of love because it's in the background, continuous, and deeply akin to one's real self. Brothers have no illusions about their respective characters, and thus are more tolerant. They are not as disappointed by one's faults as others sometimes are. To lose a brother is to lose a part of one's self that may not be given much weight by parents or lovers, and for that reason the loss is profound.

There is a huge throng waiting outside the gates to the cemetery as our car pulls in, a light rain on the windscreen. The pallbearers, a cluster of Rollo's mates, move into position. We move slowly along an avenue of trees, coming eventually to the graveside. The coffin is brought forward and suspended above the void on canvas slings. The priest reminds us that it is time to speak of things eternal and does so as the treetops shiver faintly in the breeze. Until the coffin descends.

The cars move away from the graveside, into patches of sunlight that have now appeared. People begin to chat. The tyres of the vehicles splash through puddles of water on their way to the exit gate. The world has never seemed more brilliantly and preciously alive than at this moment, which is the way he would have wanted it.

To be with him was always fun. He was Rollo.

Many others remembered him and for days and weeks we continued to receive letters and condolence messages. They were much appreciated at the time but are too numerous to be covered here. There were some of particular interest which are worth dwelling upon as an indication of the wide range of responses to the tragic events in Singapore.

One of the first messages to arrive was a telegram to Paul from the Prime Minister, Gough Whitlam:

Deeply grieved at news just received of the sudden death of Rollo. He was a young man of promise and I send to you and Alix and his young wife Jill heartfelt sympathy from Margaret and myself.

It would be excessive to mention the many other communications from office-bearers and embassies but, in the light of my parents comparatively recent trip to Iran before Rollo's death, a cabled message from the Shah of Iran stands out:

The Empress and I are deeply grieved by the news of the sudden death of your Excellency's esteemed son, Mr Rollo Hasluck. In these sad circumstances we would like to convey to you and Lady Hasluck as well as to members of your family the expression of our heartfelt sympathy and sincere condolences.

There were some letters from those who knew him in his schooldays in Canberra. Roy Morrow, who was in charge of the boarding house, said this: 'We remember Rollo as a delightful and colourful boarder together with his brother Nick at Canberra Grammar School.' David Garnsey, his former headmaster, added, 'I grieve that his life should be so suddenly cut off in its prime. I remember him well and with many happy memories, in spite of his problems with authority, and always thought of him as one with considerable gifts and promise.'

Sally's mother from her home in the Cotswolds wrote to me in a more personal way, voicing a particularly warm appreciation of Rollo's personality:

Our first reaction must have been yours – one of stunned disbelief. He was the most alive person I have ever known. The whole room seemed to glow with life when Rollo was there. I had really learnt to love Rollo in the period last year when he came to Crimscote with Jill. He was such a warm human guy, so tempestuous, forthright, appreciative. He warmed the whole house when he entered it. And who would fail to respond to a man who so enjoyed simple things like shelling peas, who so appreciated everything we did, and particularly his meals. His enthusiasm was infectious – I found myself enjoying life twice as much when he was there.

Peter Nattrass provided an equally vivid picture of Rollo and Jill on their trip to places in England, especially London:

The news about Rollo came as one of the most profound feelings that I can remember. What started many years ago as a mere acquaintance in school days culminated over the last year into a very warm friendship which I'm sure would have lasted for years. The times we spent together in London were very happy ones for us all. I like to think that those days gave Rollo some of his happiest memories.

With the passage of time, of course, the lives of those affected by Rollo's death resumed their normal course. It was easy enough to dispose of the beach buggy – after giving members of the family a few rides – but it took many months to wind up other facets of Rollo's somewhat tangled corporate involvements and general affairs. We all looked to my father for guidance as to what should be inscribed on Rollo's grave at Karrakatta cemetery. He turned for inspiration to Hilaire Belloc's 'Dedicatory Ode' which includes these lines: 'From quiet homes and first beginning / out to the undiscovered ends, / there's nothing worth the wear of winning / but laughter and the love of friends.'

And so it came about, with the agreement of all concerned, that these words were reduced to the line that now appears on the headstone with the names of his wife and children: 'He won laughter and the love of friends.'

Jill formed other relationships as the years went by and had two more children, Genevieve and Christian. She and all four of her children, but especially Melissa and Jeremy, remained close to my parents until their final days in 1993, almost exactly twenty years after Rollo's death. Paul and Alix are buried by their eldest son in Karrakatta cemetery.

Sally and I stayed close to Jill and her children too as they moved through their schooldays and began to lead their own lives. Melissa is the mother of a son, Atticus; Jeremy the father of a daughter, Mimi. I would like to think that all of these, Rollo's direct descendants, and others who knew him well, or have heard his name mentioned, would be inclined to find out a little more about him, as in the pages of this book.

For myself, in all the years that have followed his departure, I have continued to feel his presence, being often reminded of things he said and did. It pleases me when his old friends speak of him, as occasionally happens, for it means that he is still fully alive in the minds of others, and probably with all his good humour and vitality.

I have kept in touch with our mutual friends in Canberra over the years and have followed their careers with interest. Philip Wheeler returned from Oxford to become a senior figure in the Premier's Department of New South Wales. Angus Moir left his pottery in Paddington to qualify as an architect and serve as such for many years at Flinders University in Adelaide. Paul Murphy became a well-known broadcaster on ABC radio and TV. Bob Sorby left the press gallery to study law, serving as an adviser to Bob Hawke, then as a judge in New South Wales.

Some years ago, I arranged for a plaque in Rollo's name to be installed on a commemorative wall at Canberra Grammar School to mark what proved to be a happy period in his life. It is very simple. It says, 'Rollo J.D. Hasluck 15.1.1941–05.06.1973.'

Mention of this plaque reminds me that some years ago Sally and I called at Government House to see Sir Ninian Stephen, the vice-regal incumbent at that time, who was known to me as a fellow lawyer. The name Hasluck meant nothing to those at the front gate when we sought admittance, but a phone call to the main house where we were expected was enough to get us in. Later, in response to a friendly suggestion by Sir

Ninian, we took a walk in the grounds for old times' sake. Shaded by a cluster of pine trees near the vegetable garden, we came across the garden shed used as a cubby house by my niece when she was living with my parents. The sign scrawled on the door still said, 'Melissa's House'.

When we came back to Government House on another occasion, many years later, the shed had gone. Apart from some official images in the main house and a mention of my mother's role in planning one of the wild gardens, the only tangible reminder of my parents' sojourn at Government House was a small plaque in a garden by the private entrance marking the life and times of my mother's canine companion: 'Gilmore. The Friendly Basset'. To paraphrase Shelley's observation about the transience of former regimes – nothing beside the plaque remains. The lone and level lawns of Yarralumla stretch far away.

Closer to home, it is pleasing when traces of Rollo's activities appear unexpectedly from time to time. Boating friends still speak of *Aristotle* and *Red Baron*. Peter Nattrass remains a close friend of Jill and ourselves. After a career in the medical profession, Peter went on to become lord mayor of Perth. A few years ago, my son Anthony bought some premises in Rokeby Road to house his business. The street number sounded familiar so I checked my files. The facade had been altered but it proved to be Yanderra House, a building created by his uncle.

Behind it all, however, at the back of these recollections is the deeper feeling of what my brother meant to me that I tried to sum up, for my own benefit, on the afternoon of his funeral service: the shared experiences. Although close to sixty years have gone by, I have never forgotten that moment on the road to Port Pirie when two bright-eyed young girls kept peeping over the tailboard of the station wagon ahead of us, while Rollo flicked our headlights up and down, just to amuse them, and to amuse ourselves. Even earlier, I recall being with him on Claremont Jetty with our crab nets when lights on the foreshore of the bay came on and left their shimmering reflections on the surface of the glassy water. These tiny moments stay with me. For no obvious reason, they seem to mean something, and they endure.

I am reminded also of some lines from the Tom Stoppard play we saw while holidaying in Sydney, after our first visit to Admiralty House. They seem to fit the case of a traveller who went to Singapore and never returned. The fact of death is nothing to do with seeing it happen, the playwright said, it's just a man failing to reappear, that's all. Now you see him, now you don't, that's the only thing that's real. Here one minute and gone the next, and never coming back, a disappearance gathering weight as it goes on.

It is therefore understandable, I am inclined to think, that those who miss an older brother, as I do, should strive to effect his reappearance from time to time, remembering, in the playwright's words, that 'every exit is an entrance somewhere else'. And so I have written this: to bring to life what happened in the past, and to echo what was said, so poignantly, by the poet Catullus upon the death of his brother in the long lost days of the fallen but never-to-be-forgotten Roman empire: *Atque in perpetuum, frater, ave atque vale.*

And so, my brother, hail and farewell forever.

Ave Atque Vale

for Rollo

i

The dark cliffs
of Blackwall Reach

sweltering with jazz sounds,
black water...

knuckles of music on
the golden ferry –

way down in Perdido
way down in Perdido

the clarinet lamenting,
remonstrating...

crab-lanterns quietly
in the shallows

laughter under the trees

pushing away from the jetty
at Point Walter

in Perdido

ii

Hurricane lanterns, pale
thumbnails of flame under
glass canopies
tabletop fluttering with
mothwing radiance

firelight at our feet,
sand gleaming…

shellfish, the flagon,
tempting us to return

to other days, exploits,
the big stories

hindsight crackling
on our tongues, fire

burning down to steady
flame, blue charcoal,

charred lips, breathless
under the night-sky

iii

Stones rattle in the pits
on the red ridge…
children wait for dinner.

The old Chev
stands on blocks
with belted hubcaps,
harnessed to gaunt derrick
and red ridge.

Makeshift days
are rubble now, stones
flung into silent shafts.

Against walls
which once knew beefsteak
and easy boasting,
larrikin winds
come scratching down
the corrugated dark.

iv

The way into the caves
is by torchlight, fossicking
beams working deep – fracturing
the clumsy pathways.

Flowstone to the water's edge,
muscular roots sprawling
out of crevices: reflections
of the clear rock-pool.

Caves by torchlight…
glister of the water-drip
on stalwart pinnacles. Each drop,
each ripple, distant,
constant, the fragile ceiling
propped up by silence.

Knee-deep in darkness…
Flashlights whispering the way
on to the stepping stones:
my hand, your hand.

v

Supposing always
there is a coming back

a floating in from white heat

and a splash down in the sea,
the parachutes billowing,
subsiding...

supposing always
we return
from magic rafts
and darkness only

three travellers
from the cramp of space
with slow, unsteady movements
and beginnings of wise beards

coming back
to helicopter
and frail dinghy
with thankful hearts
and splinters
of an alien world

supposing always
and supposing only
there is re-entry

a coming back

vi

Craters of remembrance.
Footprints in dust.
Instruments that trouble
the moon's surface...

Ah, the quest for reality –
my boys on my back
by moonlight, looking
for spiders where the vine
clings to the eaves
at the house's corner
out there, stars…
and no end to it.

vii

The raven and the writing desk.
Indeed, a fine riddle.

Think on it.

The black raven
And the wooden desk.
Here, the sombre bird,
the desk on the other hand.

Who can unravel
love's dark language –
Mad Hatter or March Hare?

Alice, weeping in the hall,
Is older than a lifetime now
and growing younger.
Love is mushroom-handed.
She will drown in her tears.

Open the desk.
Send forth thy raven.

The ark is a crumpled toy,
The world only
a rainbow bubble
floating away from the lips
of a lonely child

into space

into the rabbit hole.

viii

Observatories. Cold domes,
those disembodied helmets,
the eyes weeping with rust
and the mouth gaping…

Beyond us, ever-receding,
the guttural whisper
lapsing into contradictions
diminishing into this,
this lantern's web
of formless shadows
and moth wings
on a dark veranda.

ix

Sandpaper whispering
to the stone. Eyes, hands,
caressing the figurine

chisel, ministering
to imperfections,
clinking occasionally and
set down.

Often, I have found you
in that work-loft, sculptor,
deep in your own cosmos –

the three-legged stool
camped in dust, your beard
dusted with grey powder,
floor criss-crossed
with moon-tracks

How can this world
hold you, old friend?

Touching your fingertips,
I feel them worn smooth
by the polishing

gradually, all traces
of identity lost
in the stone.

x

Outside the caves,
recklessly, a man,
one hand in a gauntlet,
exercising a stock whip –
the sinuous tip of that
slingshot echoing outwards,
punishing the bystanders,
ears, eyes, all senses
defending themselves…
the whip, each ragged knot,
each massive stroke,
bounding and rebounding,
vaulting his shoulders,
staggering him backwards,
the jagged sounds sent
crashing, careering
into the trees.

Beside the ticket-box,
people, brought back
from the earth's broken
domes to the sun's lash
jumping and skipping,
shattering stalactites,
stalagmites, running amuck
on the meddlesome rim
of that soft drink can

knocked down, battered
and sent spinning
by the whip's venomous
tooth – all of them,
there, congregated
in a parking area,
rediscovering the sky,
the vault of air.

xi

In the demolition
contractor's yard,
doors are propped up
in stacks – all kinds
all sizes. Screen doors.
Front doors. Back doors.
His men spread them
out slowly like cards
in a good hand, one door
exposing another door.

In the demolition
contractor's office,
keys are held together
on giant rings. There,
they tell me, keys are
held to every door
you will ever want,
or will ever need,
or have ever had,
or ever yearned for.

Strange that I can find
nothing to suit me,
that I have come away
empty-handed (his door
creaking shut behind me),
lingering for a while,

reconciling my eyes
to the gloom. Here,
window after window
after window…

xii

An ill-fated barque
near reefs off Rottnest,
a cargo of building needs,
nails, windows, doors,
at risk in furious seas.

When its captain saw
the lighthouse-keeper's
distant warning flare,
he mistook it for a beacon
promising a haven there.

And so, drawn forward,
the fragile barque went on,
went in, as if at last he saw
a faint but friendly light
above a neighbour's door.

An old anchor propped
on the foreshore now
points to the lonely place
where the barque went down,
leaving scarcely a trace.

Or points to this perhaps:
that nails, doors and windows,
homes we build or yearn for,
may come to rest at last
in pieces on a coral floor.

xiii

Darkness in space, dust...
lanterns hung from crossbeams, voices
echoing on the high scaffolding.

Beyond reach, the constant chisel
working on the buttress
and in the windless steeple –
imposing the gargoyle squint
of the old dimension on new stone,
rendering the void inhabitable.

Quaint figures, illuminations of
past and future, linger in mosaics
of the mind, inscriptions...

As you are now, we were,
And as we are, so you will be.

The dwindling world is quicksand,
molten glass, which seems to flow,
the radiant materials, images, there,
suspended in the vast cathedral.

Dust in space, darkness...
in the sun's forge, hands assembling
helmets, alloys, armourplate.

Whatever befall in the outer regions,
they will be resistant to death,
invincible, builders in space,

space-builders, with voices, umbilical
even to the furthest star, receding
and receding...

As you are, we were,
And as we are, so you will be.

legends which have come to pieces,
dust beneath the chisel…
darkness.

xiv

Anchor is a heavy word.

To ride at…
to drop.

Resting in its holster
on this poem's prow,
anchor waits –
the huge chains slumber.

Release me, capstan,
shake my chains
and let me blunder –
bundle me into the void
and by my fall
discover…

But the capstan,
the stuttering capstan,
pays out words
like pewter coins.

Haul up anchor.
Ride at…
Drop.

Anchor is a heavy word.

In a library once,
on a dusty table-top,
I wrote, Anchor…

The sun swam
through tinted windows,
my mind rocked lightly
on the surface
of another world.

Slip…

drift beyond the shelter
of these weighted words.

Never return.

www.ingramcontent.com/pod-product-compliance
Lightning Source LLC
Chambersburg PA
CBHW070858080526
44589CB00013B/1122